SHOP GIRL

www.**transworldbooks**.co.uk

SHOP GIRL

A Memoir

Mary Portas

Doubleday

LONDON · TORONTO · SYDNEY · AUCKLAND · JOHANNESBURG

TRANSWORLD PUBLISHERS
61–63 Uxbridge Road, London W5 5SA
www.transworldbooks.co.uk

Transworld is part of the Penguin Random House group of companies
whose addresses can be found at global.penguinrandomhouse.com

Penguin
Random House
UK

First published in Great Britain in 2015 by Doubleday
an imprint of Transworld Publishers

A CIP catalogue record for this book
is available from the British Library.

ISBN 9780857522863

Typeset in 11/15.5 pt Giovanni by Falcon Oast Graphic Art Ltd.
Printed and bound by Clays Ltd, Bungay, Suffolk.

Penguin Random House is committed to a sustainable
future for our business, our readers and our planet. This book
is made from Forest Stewardship Council® certified paper.

MIX
Paper from
responsible sources
FSC
www.fsc.org
FSC® C016897

3 5 7 9 10 8 6 4 2

To Mum.
How lucky was I getting you.

Jamboree bag

The smells of petrol, tea and leather fill Dad's work van as I sit beside him watching concrete streets give way to leafy greenness.

'Now you'll be polite to the auld fella, won't you, Mary?' Dad asks.

'Yes, Dad.'

'Be a good girl and I might take you to Mr Tite's if we're not too late back.'

Sweets start dancing before my eyes: rhubarb and custards, humbugs and pear drops; flying saucers, coconut snow and milk bottles. The shelves in Mr Tite's shop are lined with jars that make my heart race. Acid drops and aniseed balls. Black Jacks and traffic-light lollipops. Jelly beans and lemon sherbets.

Then I think of the pink-and-white candy stripe of the Jamboree bag.

I must be polite to the auld fella if I want one. But I don't like visiting his shop. The shelves are almost empty and the air is dead, so different from all the other places I visit with Dad.

'Surely you'll be wanting to order a bit more than that?' my father says, to men in aprons and women in brightly coloured nylon coats standing behind counters topped with shiny glass. 'There's a cold snap coming. People will be needing more cuppas this week, won't they?'

'Oh, go on, then, Sammy! I'll take another twenty packets.'

'Why not make it thirty?'

Peals of laughter greet my dad's patter. He is so good at selling tea that he's had his picture taken for the front of the Brooke Bond staff magazine. 'SAMMY'S FLAIR' said the headline, and my mother roared with laughter when she saw it.

'Look at you, Sam Newton!' she exclaimed. 'You'll be selling ice to the Eskimos next.'

As my father talks to the shopkeepers, I gaze at the shelves full of neat repetition and colour: bright yellow labels on Chappie dog food and tomato red on Heinz soups; the green, yellow, white and red Kellogg's Corn Flakes packets standing next to little baker men etched black against the crisp white of Homepride flour bags. I like the smells too: the sharp tang of cheese, warm aroma of just-baked bread and snap of fresh newspaper ink. These shops are places where the bell always pings as you open the door, the air hits you warm as you walk inside and a smile greets you.

Most of all, they are places where people chat and collect news, exchange gossip and advice, meet, greet and love – or sometimes hate – their neighbours. Even as a six-year-old, I know there is a world enclosed in the four tiny letters of the word 'shop'.

Coty L'Aimant

My mother stands in front of the hallway mirror as my brothers and sister run around her, scrambling to get on their coats. Patch is barking, Joe is looking for a lost shoe and Lawrence has started to wail.

Mum stops for a few seconds. Unscrewing her lipstick, she slicks it on with the few practised strokes of a woman used to never having enough time to spend too much on herself.

'All buttoned up?' she asks, as she bends down to Lawrence, and the smell of lipstick blended with the faintest hint of Coty L'Aimant fills the air around me.

Mum always wears lipstick but each Sunday she dabs on a couple of delicate strokes of perfume for good measure. Not a lot, though. She wouldn't want Father Bussey to think that Theresa Newton spends too much time dolling herself up. Besides, the bottle has to last. Too expensive to waste.

Dad, who smells of Brylcreem, is holding my brothers' faces steady as he pulls a comb through hair that sticks up in uncontrollable tufts the rest of the week. Then he wraps his silk scarf around his neck as Mum slips on her white gloves and gives her best shoes a final glance to make sure there are no scuffmarks on the chocolate brown suede.

'Let's go,' Dad shouts, as he opens the front door.

Michael, Joe and Tish run out in front, with Lawrence and Mum following behind. I'm somewhere in the middle and have to run to keep up with Dad. Thrusting my tiny hand into his huge one, I wriggle it into a comfortable resting place as the seven of us troop out of the front gate and down the road past the terraced houses that jostle for space on our street.

'Don't forget to look at your egg face in the chalice,' Joe whispers, as he walks beside me.

'Shut *uuuuuuuuuuuuup*, Joe,' I wail back at him, trying to push the image from my mind, knowing I never will.

'Leave your sister alone! Don't go making her laugh during mass, now, do you hear me?'

We blend into the stream of other families making their way towards St Helen's: the Maguires, the Walshes and the Quinns; the Brennans, the Newnhams and the Healeys. Gaggles of children follow in their parents' wake, knowing that nothing but the best behaviour is expected during the most important hour of the week.

Mum, Dad, Tish, Lawrence and I walk into the church and towards our pew – third from the front on the right-hand side, the Newnhams in the front pew and the Quinns in the second – as Joe and Michael go to the sacristy to put on their robes. Lawrence will also be an altar boy when he is old enough, and I envy my brothers taking part in the drama of mass while I can only watch it: the rustle of starched white surplices with frills around the collar, the smell of the incense as Father Bussey intones the prayers, the feel of velvet carpet underneath their feet at the altar instead of stone.

Meanwhile I am left to sit on a hard pew every week, knowing that for me and all the other children here, Sunday mass will be one long battle against laughing and getting a clip round the ear. The day that Mr O'Riordan put a pound on the collection plate and took back change has never been forgotten – nor the sight of Mr O'Sullivan clenching and unclenching his buttocks for an hour each week as he concentrates on praying harder.

Try as I might, Joe's words ring in my ears as I wait for the moment when I go up to the altar to be blessed while Mum and Dad take communion. Laughter and fear twist inside my stomach as I kneel beside them and try to concentrate on my prayer.

'Lamb of God, You take away the sins of the world, have mercy on us,' I whisper to myself.

'Lamb of God, You take away the sins of the world, have mercy on us.

'Lamb of God, You take away the sins of the world, grant us peace.'

But the moment Father Bussey reaches my parents with the altar boys following him, I look up to see Joe staring at me – a tuft of curls on his head and a wicked gleam in his eyes. Then my gaze is inexorably drawn towards the chalice where I see my egg face staring back at me from the rounded side of the silver cup that holds the blood of Christ. As my brother quashes his laughter to save for later, I start to giggle.

Chappie Dog Food

Michael is holding the spoon in his hand. He digs it into the tin of Chappie and pulls it out with a plop. The dog food quivers on the spoon. There's a bit of brown jelly covering it but I can see something awful sticking out. It looks like a bit of gizzard or something. But I can't think about it. Mustn't think about it.

'I'll give you thruppence if you eat it all,' Michael says.

He's five years my senior and the eldest of us all so he gets to decide what comics and sweets we spend our money on when we pool it. It's the rule between Michael, Tish, Joe, Lawrence and me. Whoever gets their hands on a bit of spare change usually has to divvy it up with everyone else so that we can buy special things.

As much as we share, though, we don't resent it when one of us gets extra. After Dad took us on the annual Brooke Bond family outing to the panto at Watford Palace Theatre last year, we all trooped off to visit Father Christmas at Clements in the high street. As children thronged, fathers disappeared outside for a smoke and mothers gossiped, Santa handed me a doll and Dad could see the disappointment on my face.

'Come on, Mary love,' he said. 'Give that to Tish and I'll buy you something else.'

Dad bought me a moneybox that looked like a red telephone box. It wasn't quite as good as Joe's, which was shaped like a coffin and had a skeleton hand that popped out to take the money. But still I liked my moneybox and none of my brothers and sisters begrudged me getting it. It's the survival of the fittest in our family from who gets the most food at the dinner table to who manages to be given a treat that the others don't.

But this is different. Michael is daring me to do something

he thinks I'll never agree to. It's a chance to prove myself, to stake a claim in the sibling pecking order that continually frustrates me: not the eldest, or the first-born daughter, or the youngest of the family. I'm just Mary. Fourth-born. No special place at all.

'Come on, Mary,' Michael says. 'Do you want to eat this or not?'

I think of the money and the sherbet fountain I can buy at Mr Tite's sweet shop, the fact that Michael will be impressed if I do this.

I eat the dog food in one mouthful.

Ladybird coat

I loved and hated my winter coat in equal measure. Just like all my clothes, it was a hand-me-down from Tish or Aunty Cathy's daughter, Caroline, and I loved the cherry red wool and black shiny buttons. My feelings, though, could soon turn to hate when my coat was hung up in the cupboard under the stairs because then it could be used as a threat against me if I played up. Which was often.

I could never sleep if Michael, Tish and Joe were allowed to stay up to watch television after Lawrence and I were packed off to bed. Mum would come up, sit on the landing between the bedrooms to read to us and kiss us goodnight before going downstairs, but I could never settle. Lying there, I'd wait impatiently for my brothers and sister to come up in ascending sibling order: first Joe, then Tish, with Michael last. How could I go to sleep when I could hear the sound of *It's A Knockout* filtering up the stairs?

As I wriggled and turned, trying to find a cool spot to sleep in, I hated that I was missing out. Lawrence didn't count because he always fell straight to sleep in the room he shared next door with Michael and Joe. So eventually I'd get up and creep downstairs towards the living room where I knew they'd all be huddled around the TV.

The house would be dark as I went down but I never needed to turn on a light because I knew every inch of our stairs. The third one made the loudest creak and I'd stretch my skinny leg downwards as my Bri-nylon nightie crackled with static until my foot hit the next step. Once I'd made contact, I'd heave my other leg down and carry on silently.

The hallway floor would be cold against my feet, just a crack of light filtering around the edges of the living-room door as I walked silently towards it before poking my head around. The room was always warm and cosy: Dad would be smoking a fag as he read the *Evening Echo*, Joe and Michael were usually sprawled across the brown velour sofa while Tish would be snuggled into Mum on her armchair.

First my head would go around the door, then a foot followed by the rest of my body, inch by careful inch. Hardly daring to breathe, I'd sneak a look at what was on telly. Why Mum never turned her head towards me, I'm not sure. Maybe it was because she wanted to let me in quietly on their evening or maybe she was just too tired to show that she'd noticed me because it would mean getting up to take me back to bed.

But Michael or Joe would always catch on.

'Mareeeeeeeeeeeeeee,' one of my brothers would shout. 'What are you doing up again?'

'Can't sleep.'

'Well, go back to bed.'

'Don't want to.'

'Dad! Tell her to go back to bed. She's not supposed to be up.'

With a sigh, my mother would get up, take me by the hand and lead me back to bed. 'You've got to go to sleep,' she'd say, as she tucked me up.

'But I can't.'

'Yes, you can. Just think of something nice.'

'I can't.'

'Well, try, Mary.'

As she walked towards the door, I'd call out to her, 'Do you love me, Mum?'

'Of course I do.'

'I mean really love me? Do you love me as much as Dad?'

'What a thing to ask, Mary Newton! You're my blood. Of course I love you.'

But however much I was reassured, I could never do as I was told and it was then, when I'd pushed my luck once too many times, that my father would use the coat as a threat that was sure to keep me in line.

'Do you see that envelope, Mary?' he'd ask, when I crept into the living room yet again.

Sitting on the mantelpiece was a white envelope with the words 'Gisborne House' written on it in black letters. I'd been told that Gisborne House was the place where wayward children were sent.

'That's the letter to take you there,' Dad would tell me.

'Noooooooooo!' I'd cry.

'Well, go back to bed and I won't need to take you, will I?'

'Please let me watch, Daddy!'

'No, Mary. Do you hear? You've to do as you're told and go back to bed.'

'But I can't sleep.'

His head would turn towards the letter.

'Please, Daddy!'

Anger would snap in his eyes as he looked at me defying him.

'Theresa,' he'd bark at my mother. 'Get Mary's coat, will you? I'm taking her to Gisborne House.'

He didn't need to utter another word.

Austin Reed brogues

I was always a little afraid of my father. At six foot two, he seemed like a giant but it was more than his height that made him such a commanding man to be around. Dad would muck in with all of us and sing along to the big band and crooner records that he and Mum continually played. He also loved to joke, and every so often I'd get into bed only to feel it rising up off the floor as Dad – who must have been hiding underneath it for the best part of half an hour – lifted it into the air with me in it.

But the closest we got to affection was when I wriggled into my parents' bed and my father wearily told me to put my feet in the toaster, which meant I could slip my freezing toes between his legs. In fact, there were so few cuddles and kisses that I remember being surprised when he once unexpectedly lifted me onto his knee as he chatted to friends.

He wasn't there to cook and clean for us, put plasters on scabbed knees or dry tears. Dad's job was to provide, and all of us knew there was a line that couldn't be crossed because his temper was finite. Most of the time he wanted a quiet life, but push him too far and he would snap. When he did, I'd leg it up to my bedroom. Thankfully it was so tiny I could sit against the chimneybreast and wedge my legs against the door when he chased after me, so he could not get in.

Not that my mother worried too much about his temper.

'So you think you're the big man, do you, Sammy Newton?' she'd cry. 'Well, I'm sick and tired of waiting for you to mend that bathroom shelf, and if you think you're not going to creosote the fence then you'll have to think again!'

My father's inability to properly finish household tasks was a constant source of conflict but my parents' making-up was always swift. Most importantly, even Mum knew there were times when she had to keep quiet.

'If I hit my head on that cupboard one more time then I'll surely end up in a home for the bloody insane!' she exclaimed one day, as Dad sat at the kitchen table, smoking a Player's and carefully filling in his books with all that day's Brooke Bond orders.

11

The blue Formica cupboard had been the subject of my mother's wrath for months. Without a word, Dad got up, walked over to the cupboard and lifted it off the wall. China and all. 'It won't get in your way now, will it?' he said, as he sat back down. Not another word was said for at least half an hour.

It was the longest period of silence that kitchen had ever known.

Dad grew up just off the Falls Road in Belfast and moved to England as a young man, working first as a bus conductor before talking his way into a job as a sausage salesman. Disciplined and hard-working, he then got a job at Brooke Bond that paid enough for him to get a mortgage on our three-bed terraced house. But that was Sam. Other people might live in council houses but he made sure to buy his own. To everyone around him, he was a leader, a go-getter and not a man you crossed.

Everything about the way Dad looked – from his good wool Crombie coat to his well-cut suits and wool-lined silk scarf – told you that he had aspirations. Austin Reed was his favourite shop – another world from the places he visited on his rounds. Instead of packets of caster sugar and tins of oxtail soup, there were soft silk ties rolled and displayed like jewels on a table. In place of the smell of doughnuts and newsprint, the scent of starch and polish filled the air.

We'd go there occasionally if Dad took us out on a Saturday afternoon to give Mum some peace. Perching myself on a big leather club chair, I'd wait for him to come out of the changing room wearing a Harris Tweed jacket or woollen

Argyle sweater, looking as much a movie star as Gary Cooper himself.

Dad didn't buy a lot at Austin Reed so what he did was precious, and nothing got more attention than his brogues. He always noticed if someone had scuffed their heels driving or hadn't cleaned their shoes. So a couple of times a week, after Mum had cleared the dinner that she'd kept warm on a plate over a pan of boiling water until he got home from work, Dad would lay old newspapers on the kitchen floor and polish his shoes so bright the leather shone.

My mother was just as immaculate. Five years older than my father, she hadn't had Michael until her mid-thirties and must have been considered geriatric for a first-time mother in the 1950s. She was in her forties by the time I was born in 1960 but looked ten years younger and her exact age was an eternal mystery. She never discussed it and there was only one response when we tried to find out.

'I'm old enough,' she'd say, with a smile.

With fiery red hair, green eyes and pale Irish skin covered with a mass of freckles, she wore pencil skirts and jackets nipped in at the waist. She was one of eight children brought up on a farm in the countryside of Northern Ireland. Her father worked the land by day, then played the violin and read poetry at night so the love of learning was in Mum's blood. She aspired to something more, just like Dad, and while he moved us up in the world through hard work, her job was to ensure that one day we'd make the most of it ourselves through education.

When Tish once told her that she'd come third in a class

of thirty-seven, my mother narrowed her eyes and asked who got first and second place.

'Look at the mess of that page!' she'd exclaim, as she peered over our shoulders when we sat huddled around the kitchen table doing homework. 'You can't be showing that to the teacher, now, can you?'

Leaning down, she'd rip out the pages we'd been patiently working on in our exercise books.

'I want you to start again and write more neatly,' she'd say. 'I'll sit down with you, shall I? Just to keep an eye. Do you want a biscuit to keep you going?'

As far as my mother was concerned, education was the way her English children were going to get on in life. There was only one other golden rule.

'Never marry an Irishman,' she'd say solemnly to Tish and me, before handing us another custard cream.

Player's No. 6

'Would you look at her? Doesn't she look grand?'

Dad, Mum and her friend Sadie McInerney are staring at me as I stand in the kitchen. There's just the three of us but at any minute Dick Froome, the grocer, or Bill Green, the fruit and veg man, may pop in for a cup of tea when they deliver Mum's shopping, maybe followed by Vic Kray, the insurance man, or the postman, who looks like Val Doonican's long-lost twin.

Our house is endlessly filled with people coming and going and the tiny kitchen, with its red Formica table and white butler sink, is where Mum holds court. Endlessly refilling the teapot and making visitors laugh until they almost cry, she offers them whatever she's baked that morning: soda bread warm from the oven, Victoria sponge dripping with jam or flapjacks oozing butter; scones dotted with sultanas, rock buns, or coffee and walnut cake. My mother's baking skills combined with her sharp sense of humour mean that a stream of friends, shopkeepers and acquaintances drop in, and the only time our house is quiet is when everyone is asleep.

'Jayzus, Sammy,' says Sadie. 'She looks a treat. You've really outdone yourselves this year.'

With jet-black wavy hair and beautiful deep blue eyes, Sadie looks like an Irish Elizabeth Taylor. Her nails are polished in frosty pink and the diamond ring that her husband Don bought her sparkles on her left hand. She is the most glamorous woman I know.

I bask in Sadie's approval as my parents' faces crinkle with smiles, and Mum leans down to shower me with kisses. It's the annual church youth club competition tomorrow and it's always a big event in our house. All of us dress up each year and I love it because it's one of the rare times that Mum and Dad do something together. Thinking up ideas, laughing some off and bringing others to life, we have all inherited Dad's love of painting and drawing, except Tish – even if she did win the Clements art competition by accident one year.

Give us cereal packets and we'll glue them together to make the Leaning Tower of Pisa. A cardboard vegetable box will be recycled into facemasks, or the inside of loo rolls stuck together to make musical instruments. My childhood is an endless battle to avoid getting light-headed from too many glue fumes.

Last year I was dressed in a matching gold jumper and tights, with my face also painted gold and two pounds of fresh carrots strung together to make a garland that balanced precariously on the top of my head. I was 24-carrot gold and romped home with first prize. But, just like Sadie and my mother, I think that this year's fancy-dress costume might be the best – even if Patch is staring up at me dolefully from his basket in the corner.

I'm wearing a bottle green jumper and woolly tights; my arms and legs are sticking through holes that have been cut in a huge cardboard box. Half of it is painted the same bottle green as my clothes and the other half is turquoise. On the front is a black-and-gold emblem that Dad has carefully painted.

Around my head is another crown. But this year it's not made of carrots. Instead, Mum has sewn together about thirty of Dad's fag boxes to create my crowning glory. I'm dressed as a packet of cigarettes: a packet of Player's No. 6, to be precise.

Needless to say, I win first prize again.

Heinz Beanz

'Would you look at your man across the road?' my mother exclaims, as she stares out of the bedroom window at Big

Hack's husband Morris, who is cleaning his car.

It was never explained to me why Mum nicknamed our neighbour 'Big Hack' although I knew that the man she called Forbus Moonery got his moniker because he spent so much time in the garden at night. Everyone went by an alternative name, though – including us. Michael was Ptang Ptang Biscuit Barrel while I was Skinny Malinkey.

'And on a Sunday too!' Mum says, as she looks down at Morris. 'Some people have no shame.'

Everything had a time and place for my mother. She cleaned on Mondays and Thursdays, washed on Tuesdays and Thursdays, and ironed on Wednesdays and Fridays. Each morning she'd go off to the local shops to buy bread, milk and meat while on Friday mornings she'd go to Dick Froome's to order the following week's groceries, and visit Bill Green to let him know what fruit and veg she wanted. On Saturdays we were woken by the sound of Dad and her dragging carpets out into the garden where my father beat them with a wooden brush.

Food also followed a familiar rhythm. On Sundays we had a roast followed by jam roly-poly, Spotted Dick or treacle tart, which we ate at a table that squabbled for space with the sofa and chairs crowded around the television in the living room. The rest of the week we sat at the kitchen table. Mondays was bubble and squeak served with leftover cold meat, Tuesday might well be shepherd's pie if there was still enough left of Sunday's joint, and the sun never set on a Friday without fish being served. The other days were interspersed with liver and bacon, sausages and colcannon mash, mince and potatoes or chops. Crowded around the table, my siblings and I kept an eagle eye on each other: no one could have more than their fair share, everyone must wait until seconds were served to make sure they were divided equally, and if you left a scrap of anything on your plate too long then someone was sure to spear it with their fork.

'Here she comes!' Mum says, her eyes widening in amusement.

Big Hack has come outside wearing a housecoat.

'Look at that auld nylon number! Have they nothing better to do on a Sunday than clean a car?'

There was no cleaning and certainly no car washing on Sundays for my parents. After mass, we'd come home and Mum would serve lunch before leaving us to do the washing-up – one clearing, one washing, two drying and one putting away – while my parents settled down together in the living room, Dad with his *Sunday Press* and Mum with a book of Seamus Heaney's poetry, a novel by Edna O'Brien or leaning her head back to rest her eyes for a 'few wee moments'.

'Wheesht stop, will you?' she would cry, if we were playing too loudly.

Those quiet Sunday afternoons were the only moments when my mother's boundless energy was finally stilled. Otherwise she lived her life in a whirl of children, cleaning, cooking, washing and chatting. Always chatting.

She looks down at me now as she tears her gaze from the window and holds out her hand. 'How about a nice cup of tea, Mary?' she says.

But I know as we descend the stairs that Mum won't be able to forget what she's just seen.

'Why she dresses those girls up like a couple of dogs' dinners and then walks around looking like a tramp I'll never know,' she mutters to herself, as we go into the kitchen.

Last night we went to Mrs Cutler's to get baked beans. It's the only place nearby that stays open late and we mostly go during the summer to buy the ice lollies that Mrs Cutler makes by freezing orange squash in plastic lolly containers: the proper ones are too expensive.

Mrs Cutler's shop is housed in the converted front room of her two-up-two-down next to Parkgate School, and the TV is always on, the theme tune to *Crossroads* playing when you open the front door. As soon as she hears it go, Mrs Cutler bustles in. Tall and skinny with legs like knitting needles, she always wears a blue tabard pinny.

There are no shelves at Mrs Cutler's. Instead a random assortment of cupboards and a bookcase jostle for space with a chest freezer where ice cream and bread nestle in packaging that's crystallized white after months of waiting to be bought.

I knew exactly what my mother was thinking last night as Mrs Cutler leaned inside the freezer to unearth some fish fingers for another customer.

'Did you see those scissor legs?' she'd said to me, as we left. 'That one has legs up to her armpits. But don't be telling that to everyone now, will you, Mary?'

Bush record player

Our home is a semi at the end of a row of terraced houses on Windsor Road in North Watford. Dad and Michael crazy-paved the front garden one summer to make a parking space for the car and there's a wooden porch with red tiles that Mum paints every now and again. At the side of the house a gate leads to the back garden where the outdoor loo, coal bunker and a tortoise named Best are housed.

Upstairs are three bedrooms: the big one at the front where Mum and Dad sleep, a middle bedroom, which belongs to my brothers, and off it a box room that's mine and Tish's. Our room is so small there's only enough space for a bunk bed and a curtain to one side of the fireplace behind which a clothes rail is hidden; so cold that we wake up to find ice inside the windowpanes in winter. The sole source of heating in the house is an electric fire downstairs, and on cold winter nights we stand in front of it for as long as possible before racing upstairs and diving between frozen sheets. Tish was once so reluctant to leave the fire that her Littlewoods nightie melted.

Downstairs there are also three rooms. The kitchen at the back of the house is filled with Formica cupboards and the endless smell of soda bread. Go into the hall and you'll see the stairs with the living room on the left where we eat and watch TV. To the right is the Front Room.

Unlike all the other rooms in our house, which are filled

with noise and an assortment of satchels, apple cores and comics, the Front Room is quiet and neat. There are two swivel chairs covered with a big flower print that Dad was given as a bonus for being the best salesman and a wall papered in bright orange. A brown furry rug covers the needle-cord carpet, and the Bush record player that Aunty Cathy gave us sits on a small table. The Front Room is the best in the house and we rarely go into it, except to play records. At all other times an almost sepulchral hush hangs over it.

It's never been explained to me why we're not allowed in there but I don't question why seven people live in two rooms, leaving one permanently empty. I can only think it's kept for best just in case the priest drops by unexpectedly.

Statue of the Virgin Mary

Religion was so ingrained in my mother that she once went to the cinema and absentmindedly genuflected as she walked down the aisle to her seat. Growing up a Catholic, she was taught to pray each night, attend church every Sunday and regard the local priest as God's earth-bound embodiment. Her family was appalled when she married a Protestant from the wrong side of Belfast and never quite forgave my dad for whisking Mum to a new life in England.

My dad took the boat over the Irish Sea and moved into a men's hostel in Watford where he met Don McInerney and Harry McCann, fellow countrymen who'd also come over to look for a better life. Soon my mother and Don's wife Sadie had joined them while Harry met his wife Sheila when she got on the bus he drove. Between them these three couples produced eleven children, who were our Irish family in England.

My father duly attended his catechism classes and converted to Catholicism before marrying my mother. But it was she who ensured that the Church was the constant backdrop to our family life, from the rosaries she hung over our beds to the miniature font filled with holy water that was attached to the wall by the front door. Statues of the Holy Virgin Mary and St Therese of the Roses lined a shelf in Mum's bedroom, and a crucifix of Jesus with a drooping head sat on her dresser. The iconography of her faith was all around us.

When Lawrence was born two years after me during a snowstorm, Mum couldn't wait for the pavements to clear for her youngest son to be inducted into his faith. Fearing that his original sin was still clinging to him, she asked the priest who came to our house to baptize my new brother, and Joe stood holding a candle beside Mum's bed to signify the Holy Spirit and light. In so many ways, her faith was the glue that bound us together, from the prayers of thanks and contrition that we said together each night before *Coronation Street* to the friendships we made with other Catholic families who attended St Helen's.

My mother wasn't one to engage in spiritual one-upmanship. She didn't bring the priest his lunch wrapped in a tea-towel or spend more time than she had to at church jumble sales in an effort to curry favour. Even so, she had strict ideas about the rules of her religion and the behaviour expected. The Rosary and the Apostles Creed were always said with a ramrod straight back, bowed head and body as still as a statue.

'Did you see that one?' She'd tut as we left church. 'Bouncing around like a jack-in-the-box. You'd think it was a nightclub and not God's holy church.'

Bending down towards me, she'd spot a telltale scrap of jam left from that morning's breakfast and pull out her handkerchief. She'd spit on it, wipe my face clean, then smile and bend down to give me a kiss. 'Now let's get home, shall we? That lamb isn't going to cook itself, is it?'

Bic biro 1

Tish is sitting quietly in Mum's chair, Michael is doing his homework at the table, Lawrence is staring lovingly at his *Jungle Book* album and Joe is snapping his fingers continuously as I sit beside him watching *Crackerjack*.

Is it any wonder that I'm the noisy one when I have Joe to contend with all the time? He makes me scream with rage because, however fast I run, Joe gets away from me; however high I climb, he goes further. If we play football, he puts me in goal and shoots balls continuously at my head. Lawrence and I are always chasing after him but Joe isn't interested. Dad still laughs about the time he was trying to teach Joe how to click his fingers and I was sitting on the potty watching them. My brother couldn't get it but I did, and he was outraged that his baby sister had got one up. I think he still hasn't forgiven me. Soon I'll perfect the art of whistling with my thumb and first finger just to really annoy him.

Of my three brothers, the only one I never argue with is Lawrence because he's smaller than me and all he ever does is smile.

'Mumma's only bubba,' Mum will singsong to him, as he sits eating his tea, and we all know how she feels.

Tish is the only one of us who isn't quite as sure about Lawrence. She was hoping for another sister to play with when he was born because I have never matched up. But I can't understand why all she wants to do is stay at home, play with dolls and continually wash the bedclothes lining their pink cot. The only time Tish ventures out is when Mum takes her into Watford to go shopping on Saturdays. When the two of them leave, I sit for hours on the garden wall waiting for them to come home, feeling the rough glass that tops it biting into my legs.

But when days stretch on for what feels like for ever, I don't want to be stuck in my bedroom. Sometimes Michael takes Lawrence and me down to Radlett Rec where we use brightly coloured fishing nets – yellow for me, green for Lawrence and red for Michael – to hunt for tadpoles. Loading them into plastic buckets, Michael leads the way home, Lawrence and I following behind, staggering under the weight of the buckets as pond water slops all over the pavements. There's usually only about three inches left by the time we're back but we put the tadpoles into an old metal bath that sits in the corner of the garden and wait for the frogs to hatch.

Radlett Rec is a long walk from home so the pull of Parkgate School – and its wide-open playground – is irresistible. It's around the corner from our house and we're happy to risk the wrath of the school caretaker, Mr Bunker, in exchange for a game of football.

Trouble is, Mr Bunker is constantly on the watch from his house beside the school.

'What are you lot up to, then?' he screams, if he catches us. 'Get *aaaaaaart* o' here.'

Most of the time we run fast enough to leave Mr Bunker huffing and puffing in our wake. But such is our fear of Mum finding out we've trespassed that Joe didn't say a word when he fell off a roof at Parkgate and limped home with a painful arm. It was only when Mum noticed him sitting pale and quiet that he was forced to confess it was hurting.

'Why's that?' Mum asked, her eyes narrowing as her suspicions deepened.

'I was playing.'

'Where?'

'Just around.'

'Where around?'

'A couple of streets away.'

'Which street?'

'Southwold Road.'

'And where on that street, Joe?'

'Parkgate.'

Joe's face turned from white to green when Mum asked him to lift his arm so she could have a look. He was taken to hospital that night and came home with a plaster cast that made me sigh with envy as I watched people scribble in biro all over it.

'Now will you children learn your lesson once and for all?' Mum pleaded.

We didn't, of course. As I got older, I always took the chance to sneak into Parkgate with my brothers and never realized that it was only a matter of time before I, too, was caught. It happened as we fled Mr Bunker, as usual, one day and my shorts got caught on one of the metal spikes on top of the school gates. As Michael and Joe ran towards home, their laughter trailing behind them, I stared down into Mr Bunker's bright red face, which was covered with blackheads as big as saucers.

'You again?' he roared, as his hand closed around my ankle. 'That's it! I'm taking you home to your mother.'

She sighed as she opened the door and saw me being dragged home by the scruff of my neck.

Joe bends down beside me now as he picks up the box that's sitting at his feet. It's the present that Aunty Mary has just given him for his birthday. Opening it slowly but surely, my brother pulls out a shiny new roller skate and brandishes it in the air, like Arthur pulling Excalibur out of the stone.

'Jooooooooooooooooooe,' I wail.

'What's the matter, Mareeeeeee?' he crows. 'Don't you want a go on them? You've got to be nice if you want me to let you.'

Joe knows how much I want his roller skates. They are amazing – long metal bars with wheels on the bottom and red-leather straps that tie over your plimsolls. I want to put them on and stand at the top of Sandown Road. I want to race down the hill knowing that the only thing which will ever stop me is flinging myself over the wall outside Chiswell Wire Factory. I want some roller skates of my own. I want to scream.

Running upstairs, I fling myself onto my bunk bed before reaching down to pull out my doll. I've never had one before. But Mum was so surprised that she bought it for me when I said in Woolworths that I liked the doll. I've named her Sandra. She has dark hair and a purple flowered dress.

Lying on my back, I pull Sandra out from underneath the bed. Someone has written 'FART' on her forehead in blue biro. Staring at her, I start to wail.

Crayola crayons

I don't know if the Swinging Sixties ever came to Watford but if they did I didn't notice it. Rainbow psychedelia didn't make it as far as the suburbs of outer North London, which were mostly concrete grey. Instead, the world I inhabited seemed full of older people from a different era, a time of war, rationing and hardship.

Some, like my dad's colleague Doug Beavis who had been a prisoner of war, had mostly left the past behind them. Doug would come over, sit at the kitchen table, laughing over a cuppa with Mum, and the only reason I knew he'd been in a Japanese war camp was because he didn't eat much of her cake. She told me it was because his stomach had shrunk so much it was never the same again.

Others, like the two elderly sisters called Aggie and May who lived together on our street, still trailed their past behind them. Having existed on the edges of poverty all their lives, they lived frugally and wore boxes over their shoes when it rained. They weren't so unusual, though, because money was tight for many people where I grew up – including my parents. As well as his Brooke Bond job, Dad did deliveries at weekends to earn extra for the mortgage. When he was once carried home because his lumbago had got so bad, my mother strapped up his back after rubbing it and he was out again the next day. For a time, the kitchen was also often filled with small plastic boxes that Mum spent her evenings packing with tablets to earn some more housekeeping money.

The place where I most felt the hangover from decades before, though, was school. While the Beatles were telling people that all they needed was love, some of my teachers still clung to values more suited to the Victorian workhouse, women and men so lacking in human warmth that their wrath was enough to make seven-year-olds wet themselves in panic.

My nemesis was a woman called Mrs Rigby, who became my form teacher when I started at Holy Rood Junior School, where all the local Catholic kids went. Until then, I'd loved infants' school – reading about Fluff and Nip, Janet and John for Miss Eccles, a teacher I adored. But things changed when I moved up to Mrs Rigby's form. In her late fifties, Mrs Rigby had dark curly hair, false teeth that were too big for her mouth, and she smelt of the peppermints that she furiously – and continuously – sucked, as if to keep at bay the anger and bitterness inside her. It wasn't enough. As her wrath struggled to find an escape, Mrs Rigby's cheek muscle would twitch with the effort of keeping it contained.

Never good at maths, I was not one of her favourites and my marks only got worse the more I came to know her. After getting a C grade, I insisted to my mother that Mrs Rigby had accidentally mixed up my work with Mary Kearns's. Mum went into school one afternoon, talked to Mrs Rigby, then took me home without a word. The Arctic chill of her anger was far worse than any telling-off and shame filled me when I realized my mother knew I had lied. My fear of maths only worsened.

Dread would fill me whenever Mrs Rigby announced that we were going to do times tables, and I would wait for the inevitable moment when her beady eyes locked with mine. 'Mary Newton,' she'd snarl. 'Stand.'

Feeling my legs go to jelly, I'd will myself to get the answer as I stood up.

'Eight times seven!' Mrs Rigby would fire at me.

Numbers scrambled through my mind before everything went blank. I stared in terror at Mrs Rigby. All I could smell as I shrank inside myself was the sweet aroma of just sharpened Crayola crayons muddled with the sharp tang of bleach coming off the lino floors. Watching the muscle in Mrs Rigby's cheek twitch ever faster, I knew that at any minute she might stand up and rap me across the knuckles with a ruler. It was the only time in my life that I was speechless.

Shamrock and ribbons

I stare at myself in the mirror. It's St Patrick's Day and all the other girls at Holy Rood will be wearing green ribbons in their hair. I have been pleading with Mum to buy me some.

'What do you want with all that?' she cries.

'All the other girls will have them! Margaret McGuire and Theresa Keating. Geraldine Quinn and Shirley Breen too. Please, Mum.'

'I'll see what I can do.'

'And they'll have shamrocks.'

'Why on earth they want to do all that I just don't know! Clinging onto the old Irish ways, sitting in pubs and singing songs. Why would people want to spend their time in a pub?'

'But I don't want to go to the pub.'

'I should think not, Mary Newton!'

'I just want a ribbon.'

'Like I said, I'll see what I can do.'

After days of waiting and hoping, I am now ready to go to school on St Patrick's Day. My hair – a chin-length bob with a blunt fringe that Mum cuts at the kitchen table because she'll never let me go to Maureen's Hair Salon with her, however much I beg – is tied in bunches. But instead of green ribbons, a couple of khaki elastic garters hang lopsidedly in my hair. Usually they hold up Joe's Scout socks but today my mother has tied them in my hair for St Patrick's Day.

'That'll do!' she'd said absentmindedly, as she rushed back downstairs to get the packed lunches ready.

'But it's not ribbons!' I'd wailed.

'And who's going to be looking at you anyhow, Mary Newton? Now, come and get your sandwiches.'

I stare in the mirror at my hair. This moment is the closest that I will ever get to hating my mother.

99 Flake

The sun beats down as I stare into the picnic basket. An egg sandwich sits wilting in the corner, its crusts curling in the heat. Beside it an apple and a piece of sweating fruitcake wait for me. We're sitting on Hastings beach on a day trip with St Helen's Church. About a dozen of us got onto a minibus at the top of St Albans Road this morning and did the drive to Sussex. I much prefer coming here than going on the pilgrimage to Walsingham where we have to spend a lot of time walking behind a cross singing 'Ave Maria' and beating our breastbones.

There are kids everywhere. Some are paddling, others are building sand castles and the rest are playing a game of rounders. They wear T-shirts and shorts or dresses and san-dals while the men in the party, who arrived on the beach wearing suits, have taken off their jackets and rolled up their sleeves. Aunty Cathy has put the lace mantilla she usually wears at mass on her head to protect her from the sun as she sits and talks to Mum. Two brightly coloured windbreakers have been dug into the sand behind them to keep the breeze off and I know they won't move for the rest of the day.

Aunty Cathy is one of Mum's best friends. They met when my parents moved to Watford before I was born and Cathy was asked by Father Bussey to look after our family because we were new to the area. She's been doing it ever since and is in and out of our house all the time, in between looking after Uncle Tom and their four children. With red hair so like Mum's that people often mistake them for sisters, her face is always freshly scrubbed, and sixties fashions are an anathema to Cathy. Knee-length cotton dresses that flare out from the waist and cream orthopaedic sandals are her preferred outfit. But then again Cathy needs sturdy shoes because she always walks with purpose as she bustles around organizing us all – along with the church jumble sale, youth club, nativity play and local Brownie pack.

I love Aunty Cathy. She's strict but kind in equal measure and I feel still inside when I'm with her. She's even promised to take me on my first ever holiday because we never get to go on them. Each year Michael buys a copy of *Exchange & Mart* and circles ads for caravans to rent. But while Dad nods and always promises to go and have a look, he never does. Cathy, though, is going to take me to Devon and she says it's full of fields, cows and clotted-cream teas.

Aunty Cathy usually arrives at our house pulling a checked shopping trolley while Mum's friend Jean Wiseman pulls up outside in her blue Hillman Imp. Mum met Jean when she was in hospital having me and Jean was having her third son, John. She is gentle, smiles a lot and looks tiny sitting behind the wheel of her car. She takes Mum shopping and the two of them also go to Maureen's once a week to get their hair set.

Then there's Stella, whose hair is dyed the colour of boot polish and has a constant smudge of lipstick on her teeth plus the poshest voice I've ever heard.

'Shall I replenish the teapot, Theres-air?' she said one day, when she was sitting at the kitchen table having a cuppa.

The word rolled around in my head so much that I had to look it up in the dictionary.

There's also Sheila and Sadie and, last but not least, Aunty Ruth, who's married to Cathy's brother Albert. She didn't even know us properly when she invited our whole family to live with hers when we first arrived in Watford. Dad had left his job as a sausage salesman and the house that went with it so my parents didn't have anywhere to go while they looked for a new place. They met Ruth through Cathy and the church, and that's the sort of person she is: kind and generous. Together these are my mother's best friends, and as far as she's concerned, there aren't enough hours in the day to chat to them. Uncle Don once told us that he'd spotted Mum talking to Cathy on his way out of the bus depot one morning and they were still there when he finished the round.

I pick up the sandwich and feel the crust hard in my fingers. Lifting it to my mouth, I close my teeth around it. The taste of warm egg and salad cream spreads across my tongue. Then sand crunches between them.

'It's baking, innit?' Mr Brown says with a smile, as he sits in his deck chair, skin slowly turning the colour of a strawberry. 'Couldn't 'ave picked a better day for it.'

Mr Brown works in the rag trade and is always coming over and trying to sell Mum clothes he's got stuffed in a bin liner. Most of the time she politely tells him that we've got all we need. Her knitting needles constantly click together in the evenings as she makes jumpers, hats and socks. Or she goes to the local second-hand shops to buy us things.

'Be a love, Mary, and get me some water, will you?' Mr Brown booms at me.

I stare at my bucket. It's bright red plastic and there's a matching shovel that I use to make sand castles. Standing up, I pick my way obediently through all the people on the beach. There are men with hankies on their heads, women sitting on checked picnic blankets spread over the pebbles and kids flying kites. Tish is somewhere sulking because her flip-flop got carried out to sea.

I bend down to fill the bucket at the water's edge before walking back up the beach.

'Lovely!' Mr Brown says, with a smile. 'Put the bucket down so I can cool my feet, will you, love?'

I stare at his huge foot and wonder how it will ever fit in my bucket. Then I reluctantly put it down near him. He heaves himself forward on his chair and pushes his foot into the water.

'Ah!' he says, with a sigh of relief. 'You could scramble eggs on those pebbles.'

Mr Brown wiggles his foot around, digging it deeper and deeper. I hold my breath until he suddenly pulls his foot out of the bucket. Then I stare silently as he plunges the other foot in, hardly daring to breathe when the bucket finally splits and water runs onto the sand.

'Me and my big feet!' Mr Brown says. 'Sorry, love.'

I watch water trail across the pebbles. I look at the bucket. I look back at Mr Brown. I look at the bucket again.

'How about an ice cream?' I hear Mum's voice say in my ear. 'It must be about time for us to get the 99s. Why don't you come with me for a walk?'

I turn to look at her. She smiles and takes my hand. Only the thought of the smooth creamy ice cream and my mother's kindly touch is enough to distract me from my murderous rage.

Bronnley soap

Apparently there is a place called Tesco that my mother Will Never Step Into.

'It just hasn't got the quality,' Mum says, as she pours a cup of tea for Mr Froome. 'Now, how about a nice piece of coffee and walnut, Dick? I know it's your favourite.'

Mr Froome sighs contentedly as I stare at his hands. Everything about him is big: from his hands to his laugh to his moustache. He looks a bit like Sean Connery with no hair, and is always slightly tanned because he goes to Spain on holiday.

Mr Froome runs the Wavyline Grocer on Leavesden Road, and my mother walks there once a week to give him her order because she doesn't drive. Then Mr Froome delivers everything in his green Morris Minor van: ham sliced off the bone and Cheddar cheese wrapped in greaseproof paper, tins of Nestlé condensed milk and Rose's lime marmalade, bags of flour, eggs and caster sugar. At Christmas his boxes are dotted with small cardboard drums of crystallized figs, Turkish Delight dusted with icing sugar and boxes of Newberry Fruits.

Bill Green's fruit and veg shop is just down the road from Mr Froome's and I feel sorry for him because he's the one that has to keep us in potatoes. Luckily, though, he has a Ford Transit van to deliver them and it's good that he does because my mother would serve potatoes with apple crumble if she could.

'Eat up your mash,' Mum says to Joe, as he picks at his plate. 'It'll fill you up.

'Have another potato, Joe?' she suggests hopefully, as she stands over him brandishing the saucepan.

But while the rest of us hardly draw breath to eat, Joe is far less interested in food.

'You're as thin as a string bean!' Mum says, as she piles sausages onto his plate. Joe stares mournfully at them. 'You've got to keep your strength up.'

Mum's desire to fatten up the thin ones in our family is never satisfied. She makes Joe special meals that he doesn't eat, constantly spreads an extra thick layer of jam on a piece of bread for me and mixes Dad an egg with milk and vitamins each morning. The glass sits on the kitchen table as we come downstairs for breakfast and Dad drinks it before lighting a fag.

Mr Froome looks at me now as he takes a bite of his cake. 'So did you like the steak, then, Mary?' he asks.

There was a fire at a local butcher's factory last week and they gave whatever meat wasn't burned to whoever wanted it. Our neighbour Eileen, who wears mini-skirts and has back-combed hair, brought a bag of steak around to our house, her Boxer dog Pearl sniffing the air as she trailed behind.

'Make the most of this, Mary,' Mum had said, as she cooked the steak while I sat at the kitchen table doing my homework. 'It's a lovely piece of meat.'

She was right. We usually eat mince, chops or liver and the steak was like nothing I'd tasted before.

'I wish that place could burn down every week,' I say to Mr Froome.

I also wish that we could try Fray Bentos steak and kidney pie but Mum gasps in horror whenever I mention it.

'What would you be wanting a pie in a tin for?' she cries. 'Next thing you'll be asking for mash in a packet.'

The one exception to the homemade rule is the odd cream cake from Garner's bakery. Mum goes there to buy three loaves every day without fail and it's just around the corner on St Albans Road. Garner's is run by a woman called Mrs Tanner, who has the biggest buck teeth I've ever seen, and for some reason I always want one of their cakes, even though they taste wet and thin compared to Mum's.

Along the road from Garner's are the butchers – Gibson's, which is best for sausages, and Matthew's, where Mum buys joints for Sunday roasts – and Mac Fisheries that she visits every Friday. My favourite shop, though, is Timothy White's because it smells of a mixture of rubber and metal and is filled with everything from mops and sponges to screws and clothes pegs. I love the smell of the place and the shelves piled high with neat rows of things I never knew people needed until I saw them in White's. Then I realized it was the place where everything that makes life easy is sold.

There is one shop like no other, though, a shop so special that my mother puts on her best cream jacket to visit it: Clements & Co. Clements isn't one of the local places near our home in North Watford. It's a department store in the centre of Watford proper, the Saturday shopping Mecca that I hardly ever get to visit, except on the odd afternoon with Dad when we stick to the joke shop, record shop and Austin Reed.

But Mum goes to Clements when she needs to buy something special, and every now and again I have been good enough to earn an invitation to go along with her. Clements is another world. Push open the enormous wooden front doors and breathe in air heavy with the smell of cosmetics and the clean scent of new stationery. The carpet is made of red wool so thick it muffles footsteps. Women in frilly blouses puff perfume as people walk past and a look of even momentary indecision is met by the arrival of the floor-walker, who wears a carnation in his buttonhole and directs you to the right department.

Ahead, a huge staircase leads to the upper floors, where you can find things like toys, menswear and lighting. But all I ever want to do is stay on the ground floor and stare at the glass cabinets filled with brightly coloured cosmetics, silk scarves and soft leather purses, displays of watches, fountain pens, jewellery and ornaments. But whenever I go to Clements with

Mum, whatever we're there to buy, there's always one display that we have to see.

'It's like springtime in a smell,' Mum says, as she picks up a green-and-white box containing Bronnley's lily-of-the-valley soap, which is nestled alongside Camay, Pears and Roger & Gallet.

Most of the time she puts it back on the shelf. But once in a while she reaches into her purse, checks that she's got enough change and buys herself a precious box.

Quality Street

Christmas started for our family in October when my mother began to store food in preparation on the dresser in the living room. Whatever went on, it was almost as sacred as Father Bussey's holy wafer – unlike the rest of the year when a war of attrition was fought in skirmish attacks on the biscuit tin.

When we arrived home ravenous after school each day, Mum would offer us all a couple of biscuits and tell us that tea wouldn't be long. But it was never enough for my brothers and they emptied the tin as fast as she filled it with custard creams, Garibaldis and Rich Teas. So, in an effort to stop us eating her out of house and home, my mother adopted a strategy of hiding the biscuit tin in a variety of increasingly imaginative places. But whether she hid it at the back of the airing cupboard or in the coal bunker, my brothers always found the biscuit tin. Once she even hid it in her knicker drawer but they found it there too.

No one dared touch the Christmas food, though. For twelve long weeks, we'd impatiently watch as Twiglets, cheese straws and Huntley & Palmers cheese balls were put on the dresser, alongside jars of Haywards silverskin pickled onions, tins of Fox's biscuits and Quality Street. Even bottles of Babycham and a small one of Advocaat went onto the shelves in the run-up to the big day because Christmas was the only time of the year when my parents drank.

In between all the shopping, my mother would bake as if her life depended on it. We never knew if the smell of Christmas cake or pudding would fill the house first. Jars of dried fruits lined up in the kitchen as Mum beat eggs, flour and sugar to make the cake, or combined cinnamon, sugar, suet and breadcrumbs to make the puddings that she gave to a succession of friends. Mince pies and sausage rolls were on a constant production line as we counted down to the big day.

'Go on now, Bill!' Mum would say to Mr Green, when she had made him a cup of tea. 'Have another mince pie, why don't you?'

After all the waiting, the official countdown got under way on 1 December when the first door in the Advent calendar was opened. As the eldest, it was always Michael's job but instead of breathlessly anticipating what picture we'd find, we always knew what it would be because Mum recycled the same Advent calendar each year. Opening the doors on the fourth, ninth, fourteenth, nineteenth and twenty-fourth, I would find a candle, a donkey, a sheep and the star of

Bethlehem. But even though the Advent calendar was hung up each year by the fireplace in the living room, a little more faded than the Christmas before, the doors standing slightly more open instead of tightly shut, we dutifully gasped with delight as we opened them.

Such was my mother's thriftiness. Stork margarine wrappers were kept to grease cake tins, ketchup bottles left upended on the kitchen windowsill to eke out the dregs, and Green Shield stamps collected with an attention that verged on obsession. When Patch ate my wooden recorder, Mum sandpapered it down and filled in the bite marks with glue. When Sandra was defaced, she scrubbed at the word 'Fart' with a Brillo pad until only the faintest hint of biro remained. I hadn't liked the doll that much to begin with, though, so I could never look at her in the same way again. When Aunty Cathy told Mum that she boiled down old bits of soap to make new bars, my mother started doing the same.

'Look after the pennies and the pounds look after themselves,' she'd say, as she peered into the pot where old bits of soap slowly melted into each other.

Christmas presents came from second-hand shops, the same deer and angels were put up on the tree each year and paper chains were made at the kitchen table. But although I sometimes longed for a birthday or Christmas present to be new, to smell the mix of plastic and paint when I opened a box, which told me that no one else had ever touched the toy I'd been given, I mostly didn't care. Because as the smell of baking filled the house, my mother made Christmas the most magical time of the year.

Kerrygold butter 1

Mum is chatting to Ula Cooper on the doorstep, Tish is upstairs, the boys are all watching TV. Now is my chance. I walk into the kitchen and over to the worktop where the Pyrex butter dish stands.

This is the best time of day to sneak a scoop of butter. Mum usually puts a new block in the dish ready for tea just before we get home from school and it will be at the perfect point between not too cold from the fridge and not too warm from exposure to the heat of the kitchen. My love of butter is like no other passion in my life.

Bending my index finger into a hook, I lift the lid off the butter dish. Delight pulses through me at the thought of the perfect block of sunshine yellow. But this time my mother has pre-empted my attack. The word 'No' has been neatly carved into the Kerrygold. With a sigh, I put the lid back on the dish.

Caramac

There are moments of perfect happiness and this is one. Earlier my mother snapped open the gold clasp on her brown leather purse and handed me a threepenny bit.

'Why don't you get something from the sweet shop?' she said, as she bent down to kiss me. 'And eat up whatever you get on the way back, won't you? Otherwise your brothers and sister will all be wanting a coin.'

I knew exactly what I wanted as I snuck unnoticed out of the house for the ten-minute walk to Mr Tite's shop on St Albans Road: a Caramac. Even going into the sweet shop and seeing all the jars lined up on the shelves didn't distract me.

Now I carefully unwrap the Caramac as I walk back home past Aggie and May's house – no need for boxes on their feet because it's a beautiful spring day – and Jack and Rhoda Evans's too. Even though Mr Evans can't walk very well, he still hobbles up to our house every Sunday afternoon to throw the bone from their Sunday roast over the garden wall for Patch. I pass Big Henry's house – he works in Budgens – and then that of the new Pakistani family who have moved into the street. Mum has been talking a lot to the lady about something called curry powder.

Mr and Mrs Dix are sitting in the window of their front room. Mum loves the fact that they get changed every evening before eating their tea but I love their Scottie dog more. Doug across the road is cleaning his Austin Healey as usual and smiles at me as the Chassel kids run in and out of their house. There are seven of them – even more than us – and Cyril and Lucian are altar boys with Joe and Michael.

Ula Cooper is on the doorstep calling for Carina. Her older brother Tommy is friends with Joe and they nearly got into trouble with the local policeman recently when he stopped to talk to them and asked their names.

'Joe Newton.'

'Righto.'

'Tommy Cooper.'

'Pull the other one.'

'All right, then, I'm Benny Hill,' replied Tommy, and nearly got arrested.

Dad, Joe and Michael are still laughing about it.

I am eight years old as I walk up the street I've known all my life, bite into the Caramac and feel perfect happiness fill me when the taste of condensed milk spreads over my tongue.

Kodak cine camera

'Ready, everyone?'

'Ready as we ever will be.'

'They'll have landed at this rate.'

'Get off me, Joe!'

'Quiet! I'm starting now! Quiet, please!'

'Joooooooooe!'

'Pipe down, Mary, or you won't watch the film.'

'But—'

'I said be QUIET.'

'Here we go!'

Uncle Tom flicks off the lights and the screen at the front of the living room is illuminated bright white. Smoke from Dad's fag curls thickly into the beam of light coming out of the cine camera. Two tiny black fingers appear on the screen bent into the shape of rabbit's ears and jig across it.

'Joe!' Mum admonishes. 'Stop it now.'

We stifle our giggles as Tom huffs and puffs over the cine camera. Then the screen goes dark and we wait.

And wait.

'Tom!' Aunty Cathy shrieks. 'Tom! The film's stuck.'

'I know, dear.'

'Shall I get us another pot of tea?' Aunty Cathy is never able to sit still for more than a minute.

Mum bends down to us the moment she leaves the room. 'Will you behave yourselves?' she hisses. 'To think that you can't even sit still at the Newnhams' house!'

I don't know how she thinks we're even able to move. Fifteen of us — seven Newtons, Uncle Tom, Aunty Cathy, their children Bernard, Michael, Steven and Caroline plus their budgie and their lodger Colin – are crammed into the living room. We're here to watch a cine film of the boys' trip to Cape Canaveral and I'm in awe that they got as far as America because we've never even crossed the Channel.

Everyone is talking about the moon at the moment. It is July 1969 and three days ago, Neil Armstrong, Buzz Aldrin and Michael Collins set off in Apollo 11 and they're expected to land at any moment. It's on the radio, all over the television, and every night when I go to bed I wonder if the moon really is made of cheese or whether Joe's just trying to trick me.

I concentrate on sitting even more still. We have to be on our best behaviour at the Newnhams' because Aunty Cathy is the boss of the Brownies while Uncle Tom is in charge at church. He's the one who trains all the altar boys and carries the cross at every service. Whereas our home is constantly noisy – records, Radio 4 and all of us – the Newnhams' is quiet and filled with books about science, geography and history. The dining-table in the front room is used only for jigsaws, and the silence is so thick as Aunty Cathy and Uncle Tom search for pieces that only the ticking of the mantel clock disturbs it.

Aunty Cathy bustles back into the living room.

'Another cup of tea, Theresa?' she says. 'And how about you, Sam?'

Uncle Tom stares at the camera, like it's a wild horse about to break free. 'This bloody thing!' he mutters.

'Language, Tom!'

'Nearly there.'

'Right. Bernard! Turn off the lights for your father.'

The room goes dark and the film flickers into life. Bernard, Michael and Steven appear on the screen, grinning out at us, with sunshine on their faces.

'It's the Kennedy Space Station!'

'Would you look at them!'

'Did you see Buzz?'

'Sssh. Sssh.'

The Newnham boys wave, and with a rush of excitement I wonder when we are going to see Apollo 11. Then suddenly a flame-coloured spot appears in the middle of the picture.

'Tom! Tom! Stop it now! The film's burning. Turn it off! Now, Tom! Now!'

With a sigh, I wonder just how long I will be expected to stay still.

Bryant & May's matches 1

The huge wooden door creaks as Michael, Tish, Joe and I walk into the church. It's dark and cool, silent except for the odd tap of footsteps as someone walks in or out. Several elderly ladies are sitting in pews with their heads bent as we file into one after crossing ourselves with holy water.

It's Saturday afternoon and Mum has sent us off to confession. While other kids play football or watch telly, we have to go to St Helen's. The church seems forbidding without the Sunday congregation in it. The only other people here are elderly Irish women who kneel and beat their chests as we wonder what terrible sins they've committed to make them repent so uncomfortably for so long.

We haven't been to confession for six weeks and dread fills me as I twist the corner of my shorts in my fingers.

'Are you going to tell the priest what you did?' Tish asked me, as we walked to St Helen's. I scowled at her without saying a word.

Tish never has to worry because she never does anything wrong. I, on the other hand, feel constantly sick when I open the door of the confession box and hear it scraping on the wood as I pull it shut behind me. No matter how hard I try, I just keep doing things wrong.

Either Father Bussey or Father John will be sitting on the other side of the screen but it doesn't matter to me which one it is. Both will talk to me in a low, stern voice about what I have done before telling me to say my Hail Marys. But how am I going to explain what happened this week?

I was always at the centre of the storm as a child. If there was a bad idea that seemed good, then I was the one to have it; if there was an argument, I was in the middle, whether I'd started the row or just joined in halfway through.

'You'd argue that a black crow was white!' my mother used to tell me, when she stepped in to calm us all down.

Mum was always quiet when it came to dealing with us, never raising her voice as she broke up whatever fight had occurred. The only time she ever lost her composure was during a row that descended into chaos at the foot of the stairs one afternoon. I'm not sure whether she meant to lasso or whip us when she picked up the dog's lead. But whatever her intention, she never got a chance to realize it: the moment Patch thought he was being taken for a walk, he started running in circles and barking as we carried on arguing. Mum looked around in disbelief before sitting down on the bottom stair and bursting into tears.

We stared at each other in shock. Our mother didn't get ill. And she certainly didn't cry.

'Jesus, Mary and Joseph!' she wailed. 'You children will be the death of me.'

But even the memory of our mother's tears didn't stop the fights breaking out again. Fighting, falling out, making up and covering up each other's misdemeanours, we moved as a gang in a world that often felt far removed from that of adults.

I tried to be good. I really did. But the energy that made my eyes snap open by about six every morning, while everyone else was still asleep, fizzed continually through me. When Mum sat me down with her in front of *Watch with Mother*, I couldn't stop fidgeting. *The Wooden Tops* made me want to scream. *Andy Pandy* bored me senseless.

The only time I came to rest was when I went to bed two or three times a year with tonsillitis. For about a week, I'd lie obediently upstairs as Mum ferried up cups of warm Heinz tomato soup or cold Lucozade to me. But the moment I was well again, my bright ideas were hard to contain.

'Let's have a go, shall we?' I'd said to Lawrence, a few days before we were sent to church, as I stared at the rolling machine Dad used to make cigarettes when he wanted a change from Player's.

I didn't dare take the tobacco. Instead I decided to fill the fag with a couple of teaspoons of loose Brooke Bond after taking the machine, some Rizla papers and a box of Bryant & May's into the garden.

'Light it, then!' I hissed at Lawrence, as he stared up at me with his big brown eyes.

With a shaking hand, my brother struck a match and lifted it up to the crumbling cigarette hanging lopsidedly out of my mouth. Then I took a long, deep drag as I'd seen my father do every day of my life. A thousand needles impaled my windpipe as dry tea shot down it and I started to cough so violently that Lawrence thought I was choking. Rushing into the house, he screamed at Mum that I needed the kiss of life.

'What are you up to now?' she exclaimed, as she ran outside to find me purple in the face.

Slapping me on the back until I got my breath, Mum took me inside, gave me a glass of water and told me that my father would speak to me when he got home. When he did, Dad sat me down at the kitchen table and told me that I should be ashamed of myself for playing with something that I had no business with.

Shame was only occasionally used by our parents as the ultimate deterrent against misbehaving. It was the Catholic Church that really drove the notion of it into me. When I was a child it seemed that every word and act in church revolved around it. You didn't count blessings. You feared sin. It was the backdrop to every prayer and act of contrition, every communion wafer and confession.

'God is watching you,' we were told again and again, to make sure we understood that He would see us stepping over the lines of right and wrong even if no one else witnessed it.

Given that I was such a repetitive sinner, I was convinced that I would never get to Heaven. And even the chance of being forgiven after confessing and repenting didn't help because I found it hard to admit what I'd done. Taking the handbrake off the car while sitting waiting for Dad to run an errand one day had seemed logical at the time. But explaining to a priest that the car had rolled back into another one because of me? Flinging my nylon knickers into the air and watching them sizzle on a light bulb during a particularly frenetic strip-tease rendition of 'Big Spender' for Tish had been funny at the time but was impossible to explain.

Sitting on the pew beside me, Joe shifts in his seat and makes a fart noise. I dissolve into giggles as the old lady in front of us turns around to scowl and Tish stares sadly at me.

'Why do you do these things, Mary?' she says, with a sigh, whenever I'm in trouble again.

Three years older than me, Tish might only be twelve but is already wise.

I bend my head. I must concentrate. Soon it will be my turn to go into the confession box. We call it the old wardrobe because it feels like you're trapped inside one when you walk in and hear the door creak behind you, the rustle of the priest's robes as he sits hidden behind the screen.

I'll have to think of something to say. I wonder how I will explain to Father Bussey what I did. I could tell him that I only wanted to try smoking, just like my dad. But children are seen and not heard; we don't do as they do, we do as they say. I think of the dark confession box, the Hail Marys and Act of Contrition that I will surely be given if I admit my wrongs. My mind is made up. I'll stick with something middle-of-the-road, like not doing the washing-up or my homework. Even the fear of God is not enough to make me admit to a priest that I've tried smoking.

Sugared almonds

While the other kids at school whose parents spoke with the same lilting voices as mine made trips back to Ireland each summer, our family never did. Tish went occasionally on the boat from Holyhead to Dún Laoghaire with Don and Sadie but the rest of us stayed in London because there were too many of us to buy tickets for.

Instead Ireland came to us through letters, snippets of news and Sunday teas with my mother's brother, Jim. Of the eight Flynn children – Patrick, Francis, Mary Theresa, Elizabeth, Margaret, Agnes, Patricia and James – only my mother and Jim had left Ireland for London. They were all each other had of home so once every few weeks, after mass, we'd take the train from Watford Junction to Euston, then walk to Jim's flat in Camden Town.

The thought of anyone leaving her house hungry was akin to asking visitors to strip naked for Aunty Mary. Arriving at her home, we'd find the table heaving with food and, as skinny but greedy as I was, even I sometimes felt overwhelmed by the amount we were expected to eat.

'Another sandwich?' Aunty Mary would say, in between talking nineteen to the dozen. 'How about another slice of cake? I've got Battenberg or some lovely barm brack. Maybe there are still some scones in the kitchen. I'll go and get those, shall I?'

Chewing as furiously as I could, I would wonder if everyone in Ireland was as fat as a house because all anyone there did was eat, as far as I could tell.

Maybe, though, it was fear that made me feel sick because Jim's flat overlooked Holloway Prison, whose most famous resident at the time was Myra Hindley. The image of her dead eyes was guaranteed to paralyse me with terror, and the sound of the women prisoners screaming at each other when we left the flat for the walk back to Euston only increased it.

'We'll take you to see Myra if you're not careful!' my cousin James Patrick would threaten, if I was being a bit too noisy.

Otherwise Ireland was felt in the frowns that knitted my parents' brows when news of the Troubles came onto the radio or in the smiles that greeted letters when they dropped on the hall mat. None were from my father's family because, as far as we knew, he had no relatives. He rarely spoke about the past except to say that his mother had died when he was young and he had no brothers or sisters.

My mother's family, though, were constantly with us in the letters she would read as she laughed and tutted to herself before sitting down at the kitchen table and writing one back. Then, after twelve long months of waiting, my aunties Peggy and Betty would visit us with our older Irish cousins during the summer holidays. Cramming into our bedrooms with us, wedged next to whoever could fit them in, the house would be filled with people.

Aunty Peggy's son Jerry wore an Afghan coat, played Donovan's 'Jennifer Juniper' on the mandolin and Mum adored him. Peggy's daughter – also Peggy – was always on the train up to London, for the markets and clubs she found there, while Aunty Betty's daughter Sheila was a fan of Camden market.

Aunty Betty was my favourite, and my first taste of heartbreak came when I had to say goodbye to her each year because I knew I would miss her for weeks to come. The reason I loved her so much was that she felt like mine for those two precious weeks when she visited. Sharing my mother with so many people frustrated me so much that I even volunteered to go to early Latin mass on Sunday mornings just to be alone with her. But when Betty visited, she spent most of her time with me sitting on her lap or pleading to play a game of Mousetrap or Jacks.

Tiny and dainty, it was hard to believe that Betty had had twelve children – the oldest of whom were old enough to look after the youngest when their mother visited England. Not that the size of her family – or what it took to keep them all fed – ever occurred to me when she took me to the sweet shop and told me to pick a quarter of whatever I wanted.

'Sugared almonds,' I'd say, as I ruthlessly selected the most expensive sweets in Mr Tite's shop.

R White's lemonade 1

I hate the telephone.

I never thought I'd feel this way because I'd spent years longing to see one sitting on the hall table. I couldn't believe our luck when it finally arrived a few months ago.

'Watford 39708,' I'd say, after lifting up the avocado green receiver, imagining that I was an operator in the phone exchange.

We were now a modern family. No more stuffing coins into the phone box for us and waiting for the pips to go. We had our own telephone and I wanted to ring Carina across the road on it every night.

'You'll not be using it except in emergencies,' Mum told us

sternly, when the phone first arrived. 'Your father will be very angry if you run up the bills.'

With that, she put a silver lock on the transparent dial and any requests to use the phone were met by a series of questions worthy of a Cold War interrogator.

'Who are you phoning? Why do you need to phone them? Why can't you talk to them at school? Why did you not say that when you saw them? How long will you be? Don't block up the line now, will you? I'll be checking on you in two minutes to see that you're finished. What did you say that you needed to talk about again?'

And so the phone sat mostly silent in the hall on a little wooden table that Michael had made in woodwork, and all I could do was love it from afar. Until today, that is.

I woke up this morning desperate for some R White's. Mum buys us the odd bottle of cream soda or lemonade on birthdays or at Christmas but today was just an ordinary one. I'd never be able to persuade her to give me the money for a bottle. Instead, I decided to steal it.

I thought it was a fail-safe plan. Going into Mr Tite's, I waited until he was busy with someone before slipping a bottle into my bag and walking out of the shop. Turning the corner, I glugged down the lemonade without a thought for Mr Tite and his profits. All I could think as I smiled to myself was that I'd drunk a whole bottle of lemonade that my brothers and sister hadn't had a sip of. Then I innocently walked back into the shop and asked for a penny on the bottle.

Mr Tite – who had been watching me the whole time through a side window – didn't say a word as he handed me the penny. I walked home with it in my pocket, feeling the lemonade rolling around my stomach and letting out a satisfied burp.

Turning the corner, I saw my mother standing on the front doorstep with a face like thunder. 'Mary Newton!' she said. 'Get inside this house and don't let me hear another word out of you! Mr Tite has phoned.'

'Ride A White Swan' by Marc Bolan

My mother was the one who read to us as children but it was Dad who introduced us to film and singing stars. Such was his love of old black-and-white movies that even the football matches that were shown on television on Saturday afternoons couldn't stop him wanting to watch the films on the other side.

A compromise had to be reached, though, because Michael and Joe's obsession with Manchester United knew no bounds. To them, George Best was a god and missing a match was unthinkable. Joe would put on his entire football kit and hug a ball during every game, while Michael was so devoted to his team that he spent hours painting every single one of his Subbuteo figures with the features of each individual player. Denis Law would be lined up alongside Bobby Charlton and then George Best would come on in a fanfare.

The decision was reached that we'd alternate each weekend between the films and the matches. I wasn't interested in seeing Manchester United play but Gary Cooper, Edward G. Robinson, Hedy Lamarr, Carole Lombard and Claudette Colbert fascinated me. Unsurprisingly, given that he'd married my mother, my father was fond of strong leading ladies, women like Bette Davis and Rita Hayworth. He loved powerful women singers, too, like Peggy Lee and Judy Garland, women with a story in their voice when they sang. Elvis was a 'handsome fella', Josef Locke reminded him of home and he grudgingly admitted that even Frank Sinatra could hold a tune. Perry Como, Duke Ellington and all the big bands were played constantly on the Bush record player.

Then one day my dad told us about a Belfast bloke called Van Morrison.

'He's quite good,' he said, and we gazed at each other because my father had never liked the Beatles, the Rolling Stones or any of that 'bunch of long-haired eejits'.

Van was from Belfast, though, so he was acceptable – although not quite enough for my dad to actually buy his album. But as the times moved with musicians, Michael decided that we all needed to start earning some money and buy something for ourselves.

'We're going to get our own record,' he told us, with a serious look on his face. '*Bridge Over Troubled Water*. It's meant to be brilliant.'

By now Michael was fifteen, Joe was thirteen and they were both earning, doing newspaper rounds or working as delivery boys. I was ten, though, and had no idea how I was going to contribute because we weren't given pocket money.

'Just do some jobs and Mum will give you a bit,' Michael

After throwing on some shorts and hurriedly eating a bowl of cereal each morning, I'd shout for Lawrence.

'Sandwiches will be ready at twelve thirty,' Mum would call, as we left the house. 'And don't get up to too much mischief.'

Our adventures were mostly innocent: games of British Bulldog or hide and seek in the alleyways of North Watford or in the old air-raid shelter that sat crumbling in Aggie and May's back garden. Sometimes we'd go up to Leggatts Swimming Pool, and once spent weeks collecting abandoned Cadbury's wrappers because there was an offer that gave you free sweets in exchange for them. Every time I walked into his shop, Mr Tite would scowl. Not because he hadn't forgiven me for my theft. That was long forgotten. Instead his patience was worn thin by the mountains of battered wrappers I brought in, having commanded the Gang to hunt them down and scrape everything from dog turd to chewing gum off them.

'Not more!'

'Yes, Mr Tite!'

'Well, thank goodness this offer's only good until the end of the week. There can't be a sweet wrapper left in Watford.'

In the summer just before I started secondary school, we got braver. Having had enough of kids' games, we decided to investigate the yards of a cluster of factories on a small trading estate a few streets away from our houses. One in particular fascinated us. It produced fur for cuddly toys and we'd see bundles of the stuff being moved in and out of the factory, huge rolls of purple and orange nylon fur that was too much to resist.

Hoicking ourselves through an open window after everyone had finished their shift one summer's evening, we rolled around in the off-cuts like pigs in swill. Later we would find an abandoned van on some waste-ground near the factories and customize it with bits that we scoured from the bins. The van soon became the Gang's psychedelic headquarters.

The Gang had rules, and the most important was that everything had to be shared and shared alike: even Carina Cooper's Chopper bike. How I longed for one. By now Joe had a white and red cow-horn bike with huge black wheels that he sometimes let me borrow. But Carina Cooper's Chopper was something else. Bright orange, with a double seat and high handlebars, it was the bike that every child dreamed of having.

Huge, cumbersome and decidedly unreliable at high speeds, even the Chopper's deficiencies didn't dilute my love for it. Most of the toys we played with had their drawbacks. My hands were permanently covered with bruises because I was obsessed with Clackers. A loop of string with two hard plastic balls hanging at either end, I'd rotate the Clackers so violently that they'd either smash off each other or my hands. My knees were constantly covered with scabs as a consequence of shooting off the pogo stick at an awkward angle and there was no soft landing in playgrounds, just hard concrete that you smacked into when you fell off the climbing frame.

The risks of Carina Cooper's Chopper seemed minimal, and the ultimate thrill was coasting from the top of Sandown Road to the bottom. Perching Lawrence on the seat behind me one sunny afternoon, I pushed off the Chopper and we started going downhill. Faster and faster we went, the road rushing underneath us as the bike got up speed. The quicker we went, the more the Chopper wobbled but I didn't care. We were going at what felt like a million miles an hour.

Suddenly the end of the road loomed and I slammed on the brakes in panic. The heavy bike flipped straight over and the tarmac rushed towards me. Then everything went black. I was out cold and Lawrence, who'd luckily landed on top of me, desperately tried to revive me until I eventually woke up. As I was stumbling back up the road, Ula Cooper saw me and took me into their house where she gave me a cold flannel soaked in witch hazel. But even though I was seeing stars and suffering from a suspected concussion, I couldn't wait to get back on the Chopper.

Blazers and boaters

It's so cold when I walk downstairs that I can hardly feel my fingers. I rush into the living room towards the electric bar fire that's fitted to the chimneybreast. Radio 4 is on in the kitchen and Eileen Fowler is talking in clipped tones as she instructs listeners through their morning exercises.

'Bend and *straaaaigh*ten, bend and *straaaaigh*ten,' she intones. 'One, two, thray, four. Bend and *straaaaigh*ten. Down with a bounce, with a bounce come UP.'

I walk into the kitchen and see my mother making a half-hearted attempt to stretch her leg as she fills the teapot and sets it on the table. 'Put your father's coat out to warm it, will you, Mary?' she says, as she butters slices of toast.

As fast as she adds them to a rack sitting on the table, Michael and Lawrence grab them.

'Where are my football boots?'

'Under the stairs.'

'And my pencil case?'

'In the living room where you left it.'

'What's in our sandwiches?'

'Cheese or ham.'

'Can I have jam?'

'No. And don't forget your basket for cookery, Mary. It's sausage plait today, isn't it?'

'Yes, Mum.'

'I've got all the ingredients ready.'

Dad walks in and sits down without a word. He picks up the glass of bicarbonate of soda mixed with water that Mum has left for him and drinks it in one go, then swallows a spoonful of Milk of Magnesia.

Gobbling my toast, I walk over to the radio and switch it to my favourite station. Tony Blackburn is chatting away and my heart skips a beat as 'Get It On' starts playing.

Mum walks out into the hall.

'Joseph Newton!' she calls. 'If you're not down here in two minutes then I'm coming up to get you.'

Joe and Michael are at St Michael's Comp in Garston now, but while Michael is doing well, Joe isn't. All he's really interested in is drawing, and his art teacher says he's very good. But Mum is too preoccupied by the fact that Joe's been caught smoking to think of anything else.

'Your brother could walk through a field of cigarettes and not touch one,' Mum scolded him. 'It's those new friends of yours, isn't it?'

Joe doesn't say much. He's grumpy a lot of the time and is either silently drawing at home or out with his friends. Mum's worried about what he's getting up to ever since he and Tommy Cooper secretly made some home brew and Joe was violently sick.

'Sweet Jesus above in Heaven!' Mum snapped, when she found out what he'd been doing. 'Will you ever learn your lesson?'

But I know she worries that Joe never will.

Tish gets up from the table and slips her satchel over her shoulder. I stare at my immaculate sister: white shirt pristine, maroon striped tie straight as a die and black Clarks shoes shined. My new school uniform is a constant challenge for me. There are indoor shoes and outdoor shoes; a tie, blazer and boater; PE kit and hockey stick. Six months after starting at St Joan of Arc's Grammar School, my socks continually slip down my skinny legs and my shirt mysteriously untucks itself; stains cling to my blazer and my boater is permanently halfway down my forehead.

Each day when I walk to the bus, I wonder if it will finally be my turn for one of the kids from Leggatts to nick it off my head and send it spinning down the pavement. Either that or one of the pupils from Durrants – girls with plucked eyebrows and feather-cut hair, boys with high-waisted peg trousers and a packet of ten Embassy – will get it on the bus. We try to get the 321 each morning because not so many of them get on

64

it. But if the 385 pulls up and we have to board we're at the mercy of anyone who wants to take a pop.

A hat has suddenly made me, Margaret McGuire, Shirley Breen, Geraldine Quinn and Lorraine Attard different. We all got into St Joan's from Holy Rood and we've crossed a gulf from the Watford comp kids now that we get on the bus to a grammar in Rickmansworth.

'Poshos,' they say, as we walk past. 'Snobs.'

But it's not the kids with Watford accents that we're different from. It's many of the girls we go to school with now: girls with clipped vowels and English parents; girls who are not Catholic and live in places like Croxley Green, Great Missenden and Chorleywood. Girls with mothers who pick them up in Volvos or Rovers at the end of the day and fathers who work in advertising or company boardrooms. Girls with names like Mandy, Debbie, Linda and Carrie. Ever since starting at St Joan's, I've longed to change my name to Cindy.

'Wub the flour into the butter and add a dash of milk, gels,' my new home economics teacher Mrs Owen says briskly, as she stands at the front of the class. 'Now just a dash, gels. Just a dash. Wub, wub, wub.'

She's almost as posh as Stella, and so are some of the girls at St Joan's. Carrie Lowman lives in a huge house in Chorleywood, and Linda Barnes talks about having 'supper'. My new classmates have guitar lessons, because they dream of being pop stars, and horses, because they want to join the Olympic team. When Sherry Lander moaned last week that we should be able to use a dishwasher instead of cleaning up ourselves after home economics, I thought she meant a servant instead of a home appliance. No one we know has a dishwasher. Although Carina Cooper's mum has a chest freezer that I know Mum would kill for.

I don't yet really understand what all of this means. All I know is that I feel different from other kids for the first time in my life and have started bending the truth to cover it up. I talk about 'my' bedroom – not the box room I share with Tish. I mention my 'wardrobe' – not the curtain covering the space next to the chimneybreast. I say I shop in Miss Selfridge – not Watford market or second-hand shops. And apparently my father now drives a Jaguar.

Bryant & May's matches 2

My feud with Mr Bunker reached its zenith when I almost set fire to Parkgate School. Michael and Joe were no longer interested in shimmying over the wall to play football with me so instead I got Lawrence to go. We were constantly together, my little brother always on my side and prepared to back me up.

'What am I going to do?' I'd wailed one day, as I stared at a cracked windowpane in the Front Room.

I'd shoved Lawrence during an argument and he had staggered back, knocking over the canary's cage, which had fallen against the window.

'Mum'll kill me,' I said breathlessly. 'What'll I tell her?'

'Don't worry,' Lawrence said. 'I'll tell her I slipped.'

Mum never knew that he had lied for me. We were partners in crime, together day in, day out.

Growing up, the five of us would make a Guy Fawkes each year for Bonfire Night by stuffing Mum's old clothes with tights, attaching it to a mask made out of egg boxes, then pushing it around the streets on the go-kart asking for pennies. On the night itself, we'd gather in the back garden and Dad would painstakingly light a box of Standard Fireworks. Until, that is, the year when a rocket shot into the box and everything went up at once. Then Mum decided the whole thing was literally money going up in smoke.

But by the time I was twelve, Michael, Tish and Joe had lost interest in making a guy so I decided that Lawrence and I should have our own private Bonfire Night. As loyal as ever, he diligently helped me to scour the local area for odd bits of wood that we heaved over the Parkgate wall as darkness fell.

'This will be much better than the bonfire in Cassiobury Park!' I reassured him, as I lit a match, forgetting that the underside of the steps we were sitting underneath was wooden.

Soon the steps began to smoke as the flames leaped out of control.

'Mareeeeeee,' Lawrence howled, as his eyes popped out of his head.

Bashing my coat against the fire, I soon realized there was nothing for it but to run and get Mr Bunker. After dousing the flames with a bucket of water, he dragged me home with a face as red as a beetroot.

'It's her again!' he shrieked. 'And this time I'm calling the police. Criminal it is. Criminal! Do you hear?'

My parents had stared at me in confusion, wondering what I'd been up to this time, until the local copper Mr Bradley turned up to explain.

'The school is going to consider whether or not to press charges,' he said, as he looked at me sternly.

My parents didn't have the money to repair the steps. I thought of Holloway, of the women who screamed there, of Myra Hindley waiting to get me. In the end, I got away with a very severe scolding and being confined to my bedroom for what felt like weeks. Even when it came to Helen Windrath's party, my mother wouldn't budge and marched me around to her house to explain why I couldn't attend.

'I set fire to the Parkgate steps,' I squeaked, as I looked at Mrs Windrath, who breathed a sigh of relief that the local would-be arsonist wasn't going to play Pass the Parcel that day.

I should have learned my lesson. I should have realized that I was only going to come off worst when I misbehaved. But although it did cross my mind that maybe I should finally grow up a bit, I had not one but two people to feud with from my first day at St Joan's: Beryl Stephenson and Mrs Duncan.

Beryl Stephenson was the art teacher. With a high forehead and frizzy grey hair, she looked like Art Garfunkel with a whiff of Isadora Duncan, given her artistic nature and penchant for flowing smock tops. The two of us were on a collision course because art had always been a source of fun and laughter at home with my parents but Miss Stephenson took it far more seriously.

Playing classical music during lessons as we silently painted, she also decided to recite 'Tyger, tyger, burning bright . . .' in hushed tones one day to get us in the mood to paint jungle animals. Standing behind me as I stood at my easel, she nervously cleared her throat and I dissolved into laughter. I was Miss Stephenson's worst nightmare and I knew it.

'It could be better,' she told me, when I handed in a picture I'd done of a battered old pair of working man's boots. 'Can you try again, Mary?'

They were the kind of boots my grandfather could have worn on his farm in Ireland and I knew the picture was good. So instead of redoing the drawing, I simply handed it in again the next week.

'This isn't as good as your first attempt,' Miss Stephenson told me, and I knew then and there that I would never be a favourite of Beryl's.

Mrs Duncan, the school secretary, patrolled the corridors in Scholl sandals and a flowered dress that covered a bosom so ample it met her waist and was forever telling me off for running or laughing too loudly. She also quickly cottoned on to the fact that I'd worked out a way to get out of lessons soon after starting at St Joan's.

There was a stream running through the school grounds that had a grotto at one end housing a statue of the Virgin Mary. Pupils were allowed to use a small green rowing boat moored there if they got in early enough before school and I loved that boat almost as much as the fact that if you fell into the river you were allowed to go and change into your PE kit. My outfit change often lasted almost a whole lesson and I mysteriously started falling into the river before double chemistry each week.

'You again, Mary?' Mrs Duncan would hiss, as I walked up the stairs covered with river weed.

'Yes, Mrs Duncan.'

Between the two of them, there were eyes always watching me at St Joan's and I rose to the challenge. When Beryl Stephenson asked us to get into pairs to do a painting, I partnered up with Moira McCann, one of Harry and Sheila's daughters. I'd known Moira all my life and she was patient, kind and usually top of the class. She was also often prepared to take part in my naughtiness because she was my most loyal friend. Given that she was a perfect pupil, Moira was an ideal foil for my plan.

'Let's do a picture of a bigger lady,' I said to her, as we stood at our easel, and soon a picture of a woman who looked almost identical to Mrs Duncan had appeared on the paper in front of us.

'Let's call it *The Large Lady*,' I said, with a giggle.

Moira knew exactly what I was up to but was so kind that she would never have dreamed of telling Miss Stephenson – even if it meant getting into trouble herself. Our drawing was soon put up on a notice-board in the school corridor, and Mrs Duncan hit the roof.

'You are so naughty, Mary,' Moira giggled when the painting was taken down and we were told off.

'Why don't I buy you some Spaceships?' I said, and linked my arm in hers.

Moira wasn't there to caution me, though, when I walked into Mrs Duncan's office one day and saw her familiar stretched Scholls lying on the floor. Putting them on a hockey stick, I started waving them out of the window. The more the girls below laughed, the more I waved the shoes. When they finally shot off the stick and landed on a flat roof, I thought I'd get away with it as the investigation into the missing sandals got under way. But in every school there's a squealer who tells and I was discovered. From that day on, Mrs Duncan and Miss Stephenson were on the warpath.

I wasn't rude. I didn't steal. I didn't bully. I respected most of the rules because I liked the structure of school. But I was a high-spirited child and could not resist defying Miss Stephenson and Mrs Duncan. When the chance came to make myself and other people laugh, I always took it. It was how I found my place and made friends in a world that seemed so different from the one I knew.

Parker pen

I stare at Sister St James. She is holding her fountain pen in her long tapered fingers. Her wimple is pristine white, her habit jet black, her eyes kindly as she looks at me. I can hardly believe that I am sitting talking to a nun about men's parts.

Since starting at secondary school, I've discovered that convent girls are like catnip to flashers. There are men in raincoats everywhere. When Miss Gains is puffing on a fag somewhere far down the hockey pitch – only blowing her whistle from afar if things get too out of hand – there are men standing by the fence. When we're haphazardly hitting tennis balls in our tiny games skirts and matching knickers, they appear in the distance and flick open their raincoats in front of girls hardly old enough to know what they're looking at. It's only because I've got brothers that I do.

A few days ago, I was sitting alone on the school bus because Tish had stayed late at school and everyone else had got off – our stop was nearly at the end of the route. Happily minding my own business, I glanced over at a man sitting across the aisle from me. With a slow smile, he lifted up the jacket on his lap and showed me what he'd obviously been waiting patiently to reveal since we'd left Rickmansworth.

My mother almost had a heart attack when I told her what had happened during an episode of *Blue Peter*. The lock came off the phone and she immediately called the school.

'So can you tell me what the man looked like?' Sister St James asks, as she looks at me.

She reminds me of the Mother Superior in *The Sound of Music*. Apparently there's a policeman coming with a book full of pictures that I'm going to have to look through.

'I didn't see much of his face,' I say, and dissolve into laughter.

Racing Pigeon magazine

The look on my mother's face could curdle milk.

'You're going to keep those things in here!' she cries at my father. 'What will we do if someone wants to visit?'

'Move the basket.'

'Move the basket! You want me to give Father Bussey a cup of tea with a basketful of pigeons in the room?'

'It won't be for long.'

'If I had a penny for every time I've heard that!'

'I'll move them as soon as I've found a loft.'

'And when will that be? To think that our home and garden are going to be filled with filthy birds. What will Cathy and Jean think? And Dick Froome?'

'These birds are almost pigeon royalty. Their bloodline stretches all the way to Belgium.'

'I don't care if they're from Timbuktu! Build that pigeon loft or I'll put them in a pie!'

With that, my mother storms out.

Having animals in the house has been a sore subject ever since Michael asked if he could bring home a mouse called Herbert that his friend Mick Rae wanted to give him.

'Mice?' Mum had shrieked. 'We'll be overrun with them before we know it. My father spent his whole working life trying to catch them. There will be no mice in this house!'

But, determined to bring Herbert home, Michael had smuggled him up to his bedroom in a shoebox and hidden him under the bed. My mother had no idea the mouse was there until she knocked the lid off the box while she was cleaning one day and a string of tiny baby mice ran across the floor. Herbert was in fact a very pregnant Henrietta.

'Bejeezus!' my mother shrieked, as mice scattered. 'Ring your father! Ring your father! Tell him to come home now!'

Chasing after the mice with her broom, she'd wailed as they disappeared down cracks in the skirting.

It took weeks to catch them and no living creature, apart from Patch and our canary, has been allowed over the threshold since. I've pleaded with Mum to let me have a monkey and promised to keep it on a lead but she won't budge.

Until now.

The pigeons are in a cage that takes up about half of the Front Room and are unlike any I've ever seen. These have reddish feathers instead of grey London ones, and Dad is hoping that by next year his new birds will have had enough chicks for him to start racing them.

'I did a bit of racing as a child,' he'd announced at the dinner table one night, and we'd looked at each other in surprise because he rarely talked of the past. 'I've decided I'm going to do it again and put a loft in the back garden.'

After buying a subscription to *Racing Pigeon* and researching bloodlines, as if he was buying a thoroughbred horse, my father dug up the grass in preparation to put down crazy paving on which the loft would stand. But after spending weeks scouring the ads for one, he'd found nothing.

'What sort of people race pigeons?' my mother would mutter to herself, night after night, as Dad sat with the magazine. 'The sort that go to the pub and wear flat caps, I'll have no doubt. What will the neighbours think?'

It was a mystery why my mother was worried about the neighbours. Mr and Mrs Dix had moved out and been replaced by Mary and Cecil, who were as common as muck, as far as Mum was concerned.

'Would you look at this?' she'd screeched one day from upstairs.

I'd run up to find Mum shaking with laughter as she looked down at Mary hanging out the washing in a baby-doll nightie. When she bent down to pick out Cecil's pants from the basket, it was clear that his were not the only ones in the wash.

'For the love of God, would you look at that brazen hussy?' Mum howled.

Cecil's Irish mam had also moved in with them. With a roll-up permanently stuck to her lip and hair yellowed by nicotine, she'd stand on the front step wearing a housecoat as she called to Mum asking if she wanted a cuppa.

'No, thank you!' Mum would shriek, as she bustled into the house tut-tutting about bringing the neighbourhood down.

She is furiously stirring a pot of mince as I walk into the kitchen.

'Taking up the garden with dirty birds!' she hisses. 'Those vermin will be in that room for months, mark my words. Just look at the loo.'

I stare at the hole in the corner of the kitchen. It's been there ever since Dad decided to bring the outside loo inside two years ago and set about the wall with a hammer. There is now an entrance to the loo off the kitchen but Dad still hasn't got round to putting a door on the hole. We are just about hidden behind the wall when we pee but there's no privacy in terms of sound. There are times when I wish I didn't have brothers.

The door opens and my father walks into the room.

'I'm going to make a start on the crazy paving,' he says gruffly. 'Let me know when tea is ready.'

My mother sighs as she murderously stabs the wooden spoon into the pot.

Oxford bags

I'm wedged behind a curtain beside a stall at Watford market. My mother is holding up a tiny mirror in front of me in the driving rain.

'What do you think?' I say.

'I think if that's what you really want then I'll buy them for you. But God only knows why you'd want to wear trousers that will surely trip you up.'

The fashion for flares perplexes my mother but I have been desperate for a pair of Oxford bags for months. Bolan wears them and I want to wear them too. If only Mum would buy me a pink silk shirt, I'd look just like Marc. My passion for him burns as brightly as ever and David Bowie is now my other god. *Ziggy Stardust* has just been released and Tish and I have learned every word of the 'Starman' lyrics.

Mum is intrigued by these musicians. Dad is confused.

'Are they fellas?' he keeps asking, whenever they appear on telly.

But those men fascinate me with their androgynous looks, skinny frames and clothes that blur the boundaries of all I've ever known. It's not just what they wear. It's the way their

clothes are used to express something that I don't fully understand. It's the first time I've realized clothes can say something
about you, tell the world what you want it to know. After a
decade of mostly clean-cut pop stars, glam-rock boys, who
look like girls wearing silk and glitter, ruffles and eyeliner,
appear on *Top of the Pops* as if from another world.

I envy my older brothers and Tish who are starting to
experiment with clothes. After turning fifteen, Tish has got
a Saturday job at Boots and I want to die when she brings
home Rimmel lipsticks and 17 eye shadows that she buys
with her staff discount. Michael is working weekends at Mac
Fisheries in St Albans and Joe is still earning money with his
newspaper delivery round, so they all have money in their
pockets. Suddenly they are experimenting with fashion as
well as music and I am counting down the days until I can get
a job too. There are 1045 to go.

For now, all I can do is badger my mother to buy me something, and I've spent weeks pleading for some trousers to
wear to Linda Barnes's birthday party. It's only been a year
since Mum bought me my first brand-new outfit for my elev-
enth birthday – a two-tone tonic skirt, orange jumper and an
orange bobble hat with a peak. But I've finally persuaded her
to buy me the trousers.

I stare at myself with pleasure. Cream with a large orange
check, the Oxford bags hug my skinny body perfectly. Lisa
Cooper, the prettiest girl in my class, has a pair that she
bought at Chelsea Girl. As I look at myself, I vow that no one
will ever know mine came from Watford market.

Fast forward a few days and I'm running around in bright

sunshine on the lawn at Linda Barnes's house. In a moment of excitement during a rounders match, I fling myself forwards to catch a ball, lose my footing and skid along the grass. I return home with green stains all over the trousers that even my mother's vigorous washing cannot get out. Bowie and Bolan would never have got grass stains on their trousers, I think, as I stare forlornly at my ruined flares.

Philips cassette tape

Sister Mary Hill walks towards the tape player. Grabbing her chin, she starts to stroke the hairs on it. She always does this when she is nervous.

'Quiet, please, girls,' she says. 'Hush now.'

Sister Mary slips the tape into the player with quivering hands. Sherry Lander snorts with laughter.

'Now, come on, girls!' Sister Mary squeaks.

She presses a button and we wait.

'The raaaaayproductive cycle of rabbits is similah to that of humans,' a woman's voice says.

She is so well spoken that she sounds like the Queen. Sister Mary Hill goes pale as she sits down and stares at her feet. We look at each other expectantly. I know a little of what is coming because Carrie Lowman revealed the secrets of sex to me soon after I started taking the bus to St Joan's.

'You mean you don't know?' she'd said disdainfully.

Carrie Lowman was the kind of girl who smoked fags

behind the public loos and had boys as friends, the kind of girl who knew all about sex and was prepared to reveal its secrets.

'Bits and pieces,' I'd said defiantly, hardly daring to admit that the only hints I'd got about sex so far in my life was seeing Sid James seduce Amanda Barrie in *Carry on Cleo*.

Carrie explained the exact details of the process in the time it took for the bus to get from Watford to Rickmansworth.

'Get out of here!' I'd squealed, when she'd told me the key parts. 'Are you serious?'

Now a class of twenty convent girls and one unfortunate nun wait for the woman on the tape to speak again.

'The male rabbit's penis becomes erayct,' the voice finally says. 'He then inserts it into the female rabbit's vaginah.'

I swear that Sister Mary Hill will have to say about fifty Hail Marys after listening to this. If she'd had to say the words herself, it would have been a hundred.

GPO telephone

Sister Alma looked like Charles Hawtrey in a habit, while Sister Frances had such huge buck teeth she resembled a rabbit, and Sister Mary Hill was not dissimilar to Olive Oyl. Sister Josephine, meanwhile, caused a scandal when she left the school in my first year to get married. To a man.

There were only two of those at St Joan's. One was Mr Photiadis, who was about ninety and taught Spanish. The other was the maths teacher, Mr Mallison, who looked like a walrus. Cracking balls at us down the hockey pitch, he'd blow the whistle as Miss Gains panted along behind him with her terrier, Brecht. The head of English, she wore plaid skirts, with cardigans and brogues, and put the fear of God into everyone because she was so strict. Miss Gains was the kind of woman who would have viewed losing all her limbs as a minor setback.

Sister Joan somehow managed to make even a nun's habit look glamorous and I always got As in English because I liked her so much. It was the same with Mrs Blainey, who taught French and was so chic that I excelled in her class. Sadly, though, even Miss de Rosario's good looks didn't make me fall in love with maths. Half Indian, she was tiny and wore red pleated skirts with matching red lipstick. She did, however, put on a few plays at St Joan's and I eagerly took the chance to start putting my private love of performance into public practice.

I had little time for the teachers who didn't interest me, though. Reciting Latin verbs in Miss Burns's class made me want to shoot myself but, luckily, she was so short-sighted that I could fling a banana skin across the classroom and she wouldn't notice. Then there was our timid but slightly eccentric Irish deputy head teacher, Sister Angela, who taught us environmental studies in a glass building that had been built as an extension to the red-brick school. When it heated up like a furnace in the summer, our lessons were constantly disrupted by her hot flushes.

Sister Angela was particularly fond of the ducks that lived

on the school stream, and one day Susan Smith, Margaret Woodhead and I decided that they should see a bit more of life. Lifting them up, we carried them to the tennis courts and let them loose. Soon a duck hunt was under way as Sister Angela had another hot flush at the thought that her ducks had been kidnapped. Once again, someone spotted me and I got hauled in front of Sister St James.

She looked at me calmly as she sat on the other side of the desk. 'Did you take the ducks, Mary?' she asked quietly.

'I didn't so much take them. I moved them. It was only a joke.'

'And you like jokes, do you?'

'Yes.'

Sister St James leaned forward with a stern look in her eyes. 'We all like jokes, Mary, and I know that you're good at making people laugh. Your teachers have told me so. But the thing about jokes is that they need to be kind. You understand that, don't you?'

Guilt fluttered inside me.

'And the reason your joke on Sister Angela wasn't kind was because she grew up on a farm in Ireland so the ducks are important to her. They remind her of home and she's miles away from her family. So do you see that sometimes your jokes can get out of hand?'

Shame washed over me as I stared at Sister St James. I thought of Mum and Dad and all their family in Ireland; the fact that Sister Angela didn't have anyone of her own in England to look after her.

'I'm sorry,' I whispered.

'And can I trust you not to make any more jokes like this in the future?'

'Yes, Sister.'

'Good. Now go back to your class and make sure I don't see you here again.'

'Yes, Sister.'

Having left Sister St James's office, I was called in to see Mrs Duncan, who handed me an envelope. 'It's to inform your parents of what has happened,' she snapped. 'I'm sure they'll be disappointed.'

They would indeed. So I dropped the letter into a bin on the way home and never mentioned a word about it to my mother. We were having tea when the phone rang and I raced to answer it.

'Mrs Newton?' Mrs Duncan's voice hissed down the phone.

'Yes,' I squeaked.

'I'm just ringing to find out if you got the letter we sent today.'

'Yes, I did see it, Mrs Duncan, that I did,' I said, trowelling on my best Irish accent. 'I've talked to Mary and there'll be no more fuss like that.'

'It really was a most unfortunate incident.'

'I've no doubt. I'm thoroughly ashamed of her. Make no mistake. I've punished her very severely.'

'You have?'

I could almost hear Mrs Duncan smiling at the other end of the phone.

'She is in her bedroom now doing her homework and I will make sure that she doesn't misbehave again. And now

I really must go because I have to take my son to football.'

I knew that Sister St James was right, of course, that I had to learn to curb my mischief in future if it was going to hurt people. But there was one person for whom I would never make allowances.

'Are you coming in for your pudding, Mary?' Mum asked, as she popped her head out of the kitchen door. 'It's treacle sponge.'

'Yes, Mum,' I said innocently, and skipped into the kitchen.

Bic biro 2

I look at the list of names on the notice-board. Everyone is signing up their parents to take part in sports day. Fathers are going to run fifty metres and the mothers are having a rounders match. The biro in my hand quivers as I hold it up to the page.

I know my mother and father will not come to sports day. Dad is too busy working and Mum will feel out of place on her own among the other parents, who are the kind of people to march in and talk to the teachers. The kind of people who speak in loud voices and organize everyone. My parents would never make a fuss like that.

While my classmates invite me to their houses and I am always happy to go, I don't invite them back. I've got a good excuse because Watford is a forty-minute bus journey from Rickmansworth. The only friends who come to see me are the ones from Watford. Girls like me, whom I've known all my life.

'You don't want to invite anyone from school back for tea?' Mum asks now and again. 'I'll make your favourite, shepherd's pie and flapjacks, if you want?'

But I don't want those girls to come to Watford and hear the Irish accents, smell the soda bread or see the half-built loo wall in the corner of the kitchen and the pigeon loft in the garden. I don't want anyone to whisper about my family or snigger in the corridor when they tell what they've seen.

'It's okay, Mum.'

She gives me a long look, then bends down to kiss me. My heart lurches.

I push the pen onto the paper and write my father's name: Samuel Newton. I know he won't come and I'll have to make up an excuse on the day that he was too busy at work. But for now I want to see his name on the board alongside all the others.

Aladdin Sane by David Bowie

'Ready, Mary?'

Michael is holding the needle over the Bush record player.

'Think so.'

'No, wait!' says Tish. 'Her hair needs a bit more backcombing, doesn't it, Joe?'

My brother walks up to me and pulls at the tufts sticking up from my head.

'Give me the comb,' he says to Lawrence, his voice so serious it sounds as if he's ordering a nuclear missile strike.

Joe digs the comb into my hair.

'*Ooooow!*' I screech.

'Stop being so dramatic,' Joe snaps. 'There's no point in doing this if we don't do it properly.'

He wiggles the comb up and down my hair for what feels like for ever before telling Lawrence to get the Silvikrin. The air around me is filled with fumes as he sprays.

'Right,' he finally says. 'You're done.'

'Can I have a look?' I cry. 'Where's the mirror? Lawrence, get me the mirror!'

'Get on with it!' roars Michael, as he stands ramrod straight, itching to start the record.

Spinning on the turntable is the latest LP we've bought – *Aladdin Sane* by David Bowie. The wait since *Ziggy Stardust* has felt like a prison sentence. Neil Young, Roxy Music and Van Morrison; the Rolling Stones, the Ramones and Lou Reed – Michael has made us buy into a record collection that most twenty-somethings would envy. I can only feel sorry for the girls at St Joan's who are either too busy riding ponies to listen to music or into Donny Osmond and Mud.

Lawrence hands me the mirror and I stare at myself. My temples and cheeks are dusted with fuchsia eye shadow and there's a huge red zigzag edged in blue running from my forehead down over my right eye and onto my cheek. My hair looks as if I've just stuck my finger into a plug socket. I look like a miniature version of Bowie himself.

'*Briiiiiiiiiii*lliant,' I squeak.

'Hurry up,' Michael squawks.

'*Muuuuuum!* I'm ready. Are you coming?'

Michael drops the needle onto the record and there's a few seconds of crackling before the music starts: piano notes overlaid with bass guitar and drums. I start swaying in front of my brothers and sister as I wait for Bowie to begin the opening lines of the song and I start to sing.

Mum walks into the room and looks at me singing. 'Don't you look grand!' she says absentmindedly. 'Now I really must get over to Jean's. There's a lot to do for the church jumble sale tomorrow.'

But I hardly notice her leave. I am lost in the moment. Michael, Joe, Tish and Lawrence are my audience and there is nowhere else I'd rather be.

Wimpy burger

The plastic table is covered with Coke stains as I bite into my burger. Tish and I came up on the train to Euston together this morning and got the bus east to go shopping at Petticoat Lane. I love the market there: crowds of people clustered at stalls piled high with everything from kitchenware to clothes. It is like going to second-hand shops with Mum to pick through things in the hope of finding a gem with the added thrill of the pressure to buy.

'Get yer purse out, love!' traders roar, as I look at plastic sandals or bottles of cheap perfume. 'Won't stay long so make yer mind up.'

On the hard plastic seat beside me is an orange bag containing a tank top with a diamond knit in emerald green and burgundy that Tish has just bought me.

'Thanks so much,' I say, between mouthfuls.

''S all right,' Tish says. 'So do you promise you won't borrow any more of my stuff?'

'Of course.'

My older sister looks at me sceptically. I am continually digging into her make-up bag and rifling through her new clothes on the sly. 'You mean it?'

'Yup.'

'Well, make sure you do, okay?'

Tish has just done her O levels and after years of misapprehension – she wondering why I don't like dolls, me amazed that she does – we have finally begun to find common ground: learning song lyrics together and practising putting on make-up, we pore over the pages of the *NME*, laugh at Cathy and Claire's advice in *Jackie* and read about fashion in *Honey*. Now and again, we also nick Joe's *21* magazine.

He is working on a building site for the summer holidays and has already decided that he will carry on doing weekends when he goes back to school for his final year. We all know that he is just sitting it out until he can officially leave. Despite my parents' belief in education, the Catholic comprehensive system is not the place for a creative boy like Joe. School is all about learning to follow the lines, not blurring them with creative thought or expression. Joe's passion for art sustains him and he has sat his A level at just fifteen. But he knows one exam won't be enough to get him anywhere and insists he enjoys the work on a building site – mostly because he has almost as much money in his pocket for those summer weeks as Michael, who has left school and is training to be a surveyor.

'Why didn't you want the blouse?' Tish asks, and takes a sip of her Coke float.

There are some things we will never agree on. I pick up my strawberry milkshake. 'You know why,' I mutter darkly.

'Oh, Mary! You can't be serious? You really think that you're never going to wear a blouse again?'

'I do.'

'But that's stupid.'

'It's not. You weren't there.'

'It was a freak accident. That's all. It wasn't the blouse's fault.'

I look at Tish. 'But it was so embarrassing!' I wail.

'I know.'

'And that's why I will never wear a blouse again. Never.'

Tish raises an eyebrow as she looks at me. 'Okay. We'll see how you feel in a couple of years, shall we?'

I mean it. What happened at Pinner Fair two weeks ago will never be forgotten. I went with some friends from St Joan's and it was the first time Mum had let me out in the evening alone.

'I want you back here by nine, Mary,' she said, as I left. 'Not one minute later otherwise I swear to God that you will not set foot outside this house alone again until you're twenty-five. Do you hear me?'

'Yes, Mum.'

'Good. Now here's fifty pence.'

I felt invincible as I walked down the road to meet Geraldine Quinn. I was on my own and off to meet my friends wearing flares with a cheesecloth shirt, which had a string of tiny buttons down the front, and a wing collar jacket. I was finally growing up.

Geraldine and I got on the bus together to Pinner, met up with our classmates and the next couple of hours were a whirl of trying not to break my neck on the waltzers and stuffing my face with as much candyfloss as I could stomach. But just as I thought the evening couldn't get any better, I saw Ian Partridge in the queue for the Cage with his brother Alan. Dragging Geraldine with me, I got in the line behind them as the Cage rotated onto its side and teenagers screamed their heads off in the air above us.

Nothing was going to put me off the chance of getting up close to Ian Partridge. When our turn came, I walked onto the ride with Geraldine and clung to the bars either side of me as a man casually clipped me in with a bit of frayed rope. Ian and Alan were on the opposite side of the ride to us and I stared at Ian, willing him to notice me.

The Cage started to spin. Slowly at first and level with the ground. As it spun faster and faster, gravity pinned me back against the bars of the ride, holding me steady as the Cage turned on its side. The world was a blur of colour and light. Geraldine was screaming beside me. Eyes fixed ahead, I remained completely silent, hoping that Ian would notice my bravery as we spun around at a hundred miles an hour.

And then the buttons of my cheesecloth shirt started to ping open one by one.

Fixed like a condemned man to a stake, there was nothing I could do. My blouse ripped open displaying my completely bare – and flat – chest to everyone on the ride. Ian was crying tears of laughter and me of shame by the time we came to rest and I pulled my shirt around me. I was so upset that I threw up the moment I got onto solid ground.

Maybelline lip gloss

'Hand them over!'

The boy has a face like a rat's, as do all the other kids with him. Rat Boy is from a family as rough and tough as they come, the scariest family in North Watford.

'No!'

'Give them to us.'

The boy steps towards me and I feel Lawrence moving closer as well. I look down at my brother and he stares at me. I don't want him getting beaten up by this lot. I give him a warning look and move towards Rat Boy.

'I'm not giving you anything.'

In my hand is a plastic bag full of sweets that the Gang just clubbed together to buy: tubes of Rolos and Opal Fruits, bags of Jelly Tots and Aztec bars. It's a hot summer day and we've all met up at the van for the afternoon. We don't come up here so often now but still do once in a while. We were just minding our own business until this lot turned up: rough kids who come up here every now and again to nick stuff off us.

'You're not having them,' I say, and Rat Boy steps towards me again.

His clothes smell of mushrooms and his breath of smoke. I wonder if he's going to hit me. I've never been punched in the face before. He curls his lip as he looks at me, eyeing up the plastic bag as everyone stands still, wondering who will make the first move and what it will be.

'You all right?' a voice says.

I turn to see Stephen Bradley – massive bike, leather jacket and a lot of attitude. He is the type who could smack anyone's face in. My heart thumps as I look at him. 'Yeh,' I say.

Stephen Bradley isn't the best-looking boy around but he's got real swagger.

Rat Boy goes still as Stephen walks towards him.

'Fuck off,' Stephen growls.

Fear and defiance wash across Rat Boy's face. Would he rather get a pasting or back down in front of his mates?

'I said fuck off,' Stephen shouts, and Rat Boy knows he's lost.

He turns and starts walking away as the rest of his group trail after him.

I stare at Stephen in awe. 'Thanks,' I whisper.

Trudie, Michelle, Carina, Debbie, the Sweeney brothers

and Lawrence start to laugh with relief as Stephen scuffs his boot on the ground.

''S all right,' he mumbles.

'Wanna see the van?'

'Yeh.'

We climb into it while the others wait outside. It's an old blue Ford Transit with a cab in front and enough space to stand up in the back. We've stuck posters on the wall that Tish didn't want in our bedroom – one of Slade because Dave Hill's monster fringe freaks her out and another of Alice Cooper who she thinks is just plain weird.

An old transistor radio is playing 'You Can Do Magic' by Limmie and the Family Cookin'.

'It's nice,' Stephen says.

I wish I'd brought Tish's roll-on lip-gloss with me. I stare down at my shorts and T-shirt. Why aren't I wearing my flares?

'Want one?' I say, holding up the bag to Stephen.

He pulls out an Aztec bar, opens the wrapper and takes a bite. As he chews, I send up a silent prayer of thanks that I left my braces at home this morning. Mum's always after me because I take them out whenever I can and often lose them. I forgot them at the bus stop once and the dog got them another time.

Everything goes still as Stephen leans towards me. His kiss tastes of chocolate. Pictures from *Jackie* photo stories flip through my head as I wonder what to do with the tongue that's furiously rolling around in my mouth. Then Stephen suddenly pulls away. 'Better be going,' he says.

I want the ground to swallow me up. I bet he's had loads of kisses.

'Let me know if you have any more problems with that lot, won't you?' Stephen mutters, as he turns to leave.

'Yup.'

'I mean it. I don't want them bothering you.' Then he turns and gives me a long, slow smile. 'See you, Mary.'

I look around me as Stephen climbs out of the van. It suddenly seems different somehow: the old toy fur is dirty and the posters ripped, a place full of bits of junk where kids hang out. It's no place for me any more. I am thirteen. I am a woman now.

Price's candles

'Not again!' my mother exclaims, as we are plunged into darkness.

Power cuts are regular now. The television stops at ten thirty p.m. and Radio 4 keeps talking about the three-day week. My father looks worried much of the time. He has hushed conversations with my mother as the two of them sit at the kitchen table.

'Where's the torch?' Mum asks, as we stare into the pitch black. 'Let me get the matches. Where are the matches?'

There's a scrabble and my mother lights the end of a candle that she always has sitting on the window ledge now. Her face looks ghostly as she stares at Lawrence and me sitting at the table doing our homework.

'Don't you be thinking this is an excuse to stop working!' she cries. 'Let me get some more candles.'

We are pitched into blackness again as she walks into the hall. There she will open the door to the cupboard under the stairs where she has stockpiled enough candles to see us through a nuclear attack.

Vesta curry

Mum puts a bowl of steaming mash onto the table.

'That'll not be enough, that bit of rice,' she says. 'So I've done some potatoes too.'

We stare quizzically at our plates. After a lifetime of mince, chops and liver, we're not sure what to make of curry. Dick Froome persuaded Mum to try it when she went to place her order a few days ago.

'It's Indian,' she'd told me, as she opened a cardboard box and emptied a stream of what looked like Bisto granules into the pan, added water and stirred furiously.

I push my fork into the brown sludge on my plate.

'What is it?' asks Joe, and I know he'll never eat it.

'Beef curry,' says Mum. 'Just try it. Dick said it was very popular.'

I spoon mash onto my plate and mix it into the curry, which is oozing water, the sauce separating quickly and leaving a watery trail underneath the rice. As Mum eats determinedly, Dad digs his fork into the food, raises it to his lips and opens his mouth. If he could hold his nose and swallow at this second then I'm sure he would.

But it's 1974 and the world is changing. Even in Watford. Mum's started wearing mustard slacks, people are eating something called chicken chow mein and the sweet shop is being run by Mr Hussein, who is from Pakistan, now that Mr Tite has retired. At home things are on the move too. Tish has started going out in the evenings with friends like Khalid and Zephyr, who make me gasp in admiration because they wear five-button Oxford bags. I'm filled with envy at the freedom my sister has as I walk to the church youth club or sit at home with Mum and Dad.

'You can go out to a market for the day but you're fourteen and certainly not old enough yet to be going to pubs,' Mum tells me, as I plead with her to let me go out with Tish. 'We don't want the police here again, now, do we?'

'But Tish will make me up to look older,' I say. 'Everyone says I look at least sixteen.'

'Well, you're not, and I'm not letting you out to get up to God knows what shenanigans.'

I stare dolefully at my mother as the contestants stand in front of the conveyor-belt on *The Generation Game* trying to memorize the line passing in front of them: a carpet cleaner and a case of champagne, an egg boiler and matching suitcases, a drill and the cuddly toy. It's usually my favourite bit of the programme but tonight I want to be anywhere but at home.

'Shall I get us some Angel Delight?' Mum asks.

I look at her, wanting to carry on arguing, knowing I'll never win the battle.

'Okay,' I say, and she smiles.

'You're a good girl, aren't you, Mary?' she says, as she gets up.

There is a definite distinction between good and bad girls for my mother. Good girls stay at home, study hard and are sensible when they go out. Tish is a good girl and that is why my parents let her. But bad girls' heads are turned by boys, alcohol and discos, and the jury is still out on which path I'm to follow after all the pranks I've played at school.

'Did you see what happened to her?' my father said to me not long ago, after we'd watched a documentary called *Dummy* that featured a prostitute. 'She ended up a hoor.'

He'd stared at me intently and I'd gazed back at him in confusion. I knew he was worried but did he really think I'd end up a prostitute?

'You must never let a boy touch you down there,' Mum whispers, in a low voice every now and again. 'Not until you're married, that is.'

Despite my kiss with Stephen Bradley and the best efforts of Carrie Lowman and Sister Mary Hill, I still hadn't made proper head or tail of sex until a boy called Eugene gave me another envelope as I got onto the school bus. Eugene went to a local grammar school and had started writing me love letters soon after we met. He was tall and slim, and my heart raced whenever he looked at me. But the last envelope he gave me didn't contain a love letter. Instead I'd opened it to find a piece of A4 on which he'd painstakingly stuck tiny pictures he'd photocopied out of *Kama Sutra*.

I'd stared at the drawings in astonishment before taking the envelope home and handing it to Mum, who I hoped might explain. Given that I had never seen my parents naked, and their attitude to nudity had somehow convinced me that wearing navy knickers in the bath was appropriate, I should not have been surprised when she pursed her lips and wordlessly ripped the letter to shreds. The next day I found Mum waiting for me at the bus stop. Eugene had just winked at me on the 321 when I glanced down to see Mum on the pavement. As we got off the bus, she'd fixed Eugene with such a look of disgust that he hadn't dared glance in my direction again.

With a sigh, I dig my fork into the curry and eat a mouthful before looking at Mum. 'Is it supposed to be crunchy?' I ask.

'I'm not quite sure,' she replies. 'Now just eat up.'

Boots 17 mascara

I'm tied to a stake and a girl from the fifth year is kneeling in front of me.

'God be with you, Joan,' she says, as she bends her head.

It's the final moments of *Saint Joan* and I'm ready to pour every last dreg of emotion into George Bernard Shaw's closing scene. We have a new drama teacher called Mr Harold and he's taken a chance on giving me the lead in the school play – it normally goes to an older girl. I was worried he might give the part to Katy Hill because she's my main competition. She reads Harold Pinter in her spare time and is so bright she's always top of the class.

I take a deep breath as I stare out into the audience. I know Mum and Dad are sitting in the school hall somewhere but I can't see them. The lights are too bright and, besides, I am Joan of Arc. I am about to be burned at the stake. My loyal followers are crowding around me wearing tabards made of sacking.

I am wearing one, too, but have taken a few liberties with the rest of my costume. Instead of looking like a dowdy saint, my eyelashes are slathered in Boots 17 mascara and there's a light dusting of Max Factor glitter powder on my cheeks. I wanted to look half decent for my big moment because I've never felt so myself as I have since starting to act in the drama club. It's a new thing for St Joan's. The nuns hadn't made too much of theatre until Mr Harold arrived and started the club.

He looks a bit like a young Peter Sellers in the battered old cords and pale blue shirts that he wears with oxblood-coloured brogues. He and his wife – who's also teaching here – have decreased the average age of the teachers at St Joan's by about thirty years and I adore them. Mr Harold in particular, though. Soon after he started the drama club, I'd said something or other to Geraldine Quinn when I'd been the one in charge of rehearsing some lines and she'd told me that I was bossy.

'Mr Ha*rrrrrooooooold*,' I'd wailed. 'Geraldine thinks I'm bossy. I'm not bossy! But what else can I do but tell her? We can't do this scene if she hasn't learned her lines.'

He'd taken me outside the school hall where we were rehearsing and into the corridor where he'd fixed me with a steady gaze. 'You need to listen to me, Mary,' he'd said. 'You're a leader even if you don't know it yet. But you can't boss and dictate to people. You have to learn to lead with charm.'

I had no idea what he meant but it sounded nice.

I love performing: the thrill of having an audience, the vibration in the room, learning words and lines, the beat, the timing. My mother's love of books and poetry and my father's of dancing and music have condensed inside me and I know instinctively when to drop a funny aside or let words hang in the air during a sad scene. It comes naturally to me and, after a lifetime in the midst of all my siblings, I am suddenly the best at something.

So here I am: about to go up in smoke but ready to deliver my final rousing speech. The fifth-year girl bends her head even lower. I wait for her to raise it again so I can utter my final piece of saintly wisdom before the fire is lit. I wait. And I wait. And then I stare down in confusion.

The girl is tugging her head furiously but can't raise it. She bobs up and down, her cheeks going more purple by the second with the effort. But no matter how hard she tries, she can't get free. Her crucifix has fallen between a gap in the stage floorboards and she's stuck.

There's nothing else to do. The show must go on.

'Joan, Joan,' my followers keen, as Sister Alma turns on the orange lights that illuminate the pile of wood I'm tied to.

I deliver my final line as Sister Frances puffs smoke across the stage and I stare into the distance. I am going willingly into the arms of God. I am St Joan. I fix a beatific smile on my face as smoke fills my eyes and my mascara starts to run in black puddles down my cheeks.

But all I can think of is the fifth-year kneeling in front of me with her arse in the air as the stage falls dark and the applause starts. I was never any good at being upstaged.

Embassy Number 1

I stare out of the bathroom window as I take a drag on the cigarette. I come here every now and again when everyone is out. Mum's gone shopping with Tish; Joe and Michael are working and Lawrence is out with his friends. I either nick the fag butts that Dad leaves in his garden jacket or take cigarettes out of the packets that Joe hides behind the piano.

'If you tell then so will I,' I wrote on a piece of paper that I stuck in the packet when I first discovered the cigarettes.

Joe has remained silent and so have I.

I sigh. I am all alone. Stuck here when I want to be on a stage in London or Paris. I want adventure. I want to see the world. Instead all I can see is the rooftops of North Watford's terraces.

I hear footsteps on the stairs. Smoke streams out of my mouth as I wave my hand in front of it and run panicking into my bedroom with the lit cigarette in my hand. Looking from left to right as heavy feet stride towards my door, I flick the cigarette and it sails down the back of the dressing-table.

Michael walks into the room. 'What are you doing?'

'Nothing.'

'Doesn't seem like nothing.'

'Honest. Nothing.'

All I can think of is the lit fag that's down the back of the dressing-table. If I don't get Michael out of here quickly, the house will burn down. And then I'll be in real trouble.

'I'm sure I can smell smoke,' he says.

'Really?'

'Yes.'

'Dad must have had one.'

'He's been at the pigeon club since nine, Mary.'

'Perhaps the smoke blew in through the window.'

I stare at Michael. I know he's never going to let me off the hook.

'Oh, all right, then!' I wail, as I fling myself towards the dressing-table. 'It's me. But please don't tell.'

I scrabble behind the dressing-table as Michael walks out. Whether he tells or not will not matter. In a matter of weeks, the drainpipe at the back of the house will get blocked and my father will gaze in bewilderment as he digs out all the butts I've thrown down it.

Granny Smith apples

Susan Smith, Margaret Woodhead and I are standing in the art room having snuck in during the lunch break. There's a charity concert being put on and I don't have the money for a ticket so I've decided to forge one with Susan and Margaret's help. We know the tickets were made with orange card that's stored in the art-supplies cupboard so now we just have to find it.

A huge bowl of fruit is standing on a white-clothed table in the middle of the art room. It looks so delicious that I help myself to a Granny Smith on the way to the cupboard. Then some grapes and a pear followed by a banana on the way back. Susan and Margaret join in. We stuff our faces and pockets with fruit, leaving just a few pips and cores lying on the table as we sneak away with the orange card.

'It's only a bit of fruit,' I say, with a giggle, as we scarper.

Trouble is, the fruit is in fact the still-life for the art A-level exam due to start about fifteen minutes later. Miss Stephenson almost has a fainting fit and I get hauled up in front of Sister St James.

'We meet again,' she says, as I sit down in front of her.

Her right eyebrow arches just a fraction. Shame fills me.

'So you're in trouble with Miss Stephenson?' she says.

'Yes, Sister.'

'This is very unfortunate.'

'Yes, Sister.'

'As you know, there were several pupils preparing to sit an important exam and you have caused a great deal of trouble for them and Miss Stephenson.'

'Yes, Sister. I'm sorry.'

Sister St James leans back and looks at me. 'So why did you eat the still-life, Mary?'

'I don't know.'

'Well, you must know. There must have been a reason.'

I stare at her, scrambling to find an excuse. 'I was hungry,' I blurt out.

'Hungry?'

'Yes.'

'Be that as it may, it is against the rules to break into classrooms, and disrespectful to eat food that is not yours. Do you understand?'

'Yes, Sister.'

'This is not the first time you've been in to see me but you're no longer a child. You're growing up now, Mary, and you really must learn to follow the rules. Do you understand?'

'Yes, Sister.'

'The thing about rules is that we need them because we are a family here at St Joan's. Rules are important. They are what give us structure and discipline. You must follow rules in your family?'

'Yes, Sister.'

'Then you will know they must be respected. I trust that you will remember this conversation in future.'

I look at Sister St James. Like my mother and Aunty Cathy, she's a woman I know not to disobey. 'Yes, Sister.'

'Good. You cannot keep being sent to see me. Please make sure that this does not happen again. But for now we have another problem because Miss Stephenson has decided that she can no longer teach you.'

I gulp. 'Really?'

'Yes. She feels that you are too disruptive. So disruptive, in fact, that she cannot have you in her class. This really is a most unusual situation.' Sister St James gives me a long look.

'So what we are going to do is this: from now on, instead of going to your art class, you will come and see me each week and we will read poetry together. I'm afraid that I'm really not very good at art.'

Elation and panic mix inside me. No more Miss Stephenson. But two hours a week alone with the headmistress?

I shuffle out of the office hanging my head in shame. Mum will be furious when she hears about this and, sure enough, the air is icy when I arrive home later that afternoon to find the tea table laden with soda bread and cakes.

'So I'm not feeding you enough, am I?' my mother says, her fury dripping through every syllable. 'You go to school hungry, do you now, Mary Newton?'

I can't say a word.

The next day I line up for assembly and the headmistress stands up in front of the whole school.

'As some of you will know, there was an unfortunate incident in the art room yesterday,' she says. 'It has now been dealt with but all I'd like to say is that if any pupil is ever hungry then you can always go to the sick bay where there will be things to eat.'

I want the ground to swallow me up, to disappear in a puddle, like the Wicked Witch in *The Wizard of Oz*. Banned from the art class, and the talk of the entire school, I am also now the starving Irish kid with a mother who refuses to speak to her. From across the hall, Tish fixes me with a sorry look.

Mills & Boon

The pigeon loft was the nerve centre of Dad's racing ambitions and no one in the neighbourhood could have doubted it. Standing ten feet high by ten feet wide, the loft looked like the Post Office Tower and my mother would gaze forlornly at it as she stood at the sink doing the washing-up.

Within weeks of the first chicks hatching, they were encouraged to explore. First they were moved to a larger section of the loft, where they learned to find the food and water Dad had left out for them. Then they were allowed into the garden and were soon taking off on short flights, developing their homing instincts bit by bit as they flew further.

Pacing the garden, like an expectant father waiting for the birth of his first child, Dad would wait nervously until the birds came home. But his confidence grew with theirs and soon he started loading the birds into a basket and driving them out into the countryside where he would release them. Each week he drove a little further to teach them to fly increasingly longer distances.

Once he started racing the birds, they were flown each week, and on Friday nights Dad would go down to drop off the pigeons at his club. The birds were then loaded onto a truck, taken out to the race point and Dad spent the whole of Saturday pacing around as he compulsively checked his watch.

'Where are they?' he'd huff, as he walked out into the garden to stare at an empty sky.

But eventually they'd get home and Dad would check their tags and log their flying times as faithfully as he'd once kept notes on his Brooke Bond orders.

Not that he had to any more. My father had been made redundant and bought himself a Rover with his pay-off plus a new washing-machine to replace Mum's old twin tub in an effort to appease her about the pigeons. Thankfully, unemployment proved a temporary blip because he soon found a job as the stock controller at Clements.

As obsessed as Dad was with his birds, though, the rest of us weren't that interested in his racing ambitions and were only reluctantly dragged into them.

'Don't forget the basket!' he'd call some mornings to Michael, as my brother walked downstairs ready to go to work in his pristine suit.

With a grimace on his face, Michael would load the pigeon basket into his Opel Ascona, drive the birds into a field near Tring on his way to the office and then tramp into the mud to release them.

The only one of us who had any time for the pigeons was Joe, who had now left school and was working full-time on a building site. Mum's distress as she watched him leave for work each day was almost palpable because Joe was as unsuited to being on a building site as he had been to a classroom. Arriving home at the end of each day so exhausted that he almost fell asleep as he ate, his hands were covered with sore patches and his hair full of dust. My mother would sigh as she spooned potatoes onto his plate and we all knew her worry still weighed heavy.

But while she tried to disguise her concern for Joe, Mum's disdain for Dad's hobby was all too apparent – and only got worse with the arrival of the friends he made through pigeon racing. Down-to-earth and good-natured men, they were still not good enough for Mum. She would go silent when Jack Davis, a former merchant seaman, who never wore anything on his feet but plimsolls because a life on the ocean had not equipped him for brogues, arrived at the house to spend hours talking to Dad about taggings, timings and training schedules. Or instead of loading the table as she did for every other visitor, she'd grudgingly put out a single cake when Arthur, a tiny northern man, came over with his wife Gladys, whose slightly macho exterior hid a heart that beat for romance.

'So do you like Mills & Boon, Theresa?' she asked innocently one day, over tea.

I could almost see my mother forcing her eyeballs not to roll upwards in disgust. 'I haven't read any,' she replied evenly.

'You'd like to, though, wouldn't you, Mum?' Joe put in. 'You're always saying you'd like to read some.'

As we sniggered into our teacups, my mother grimaced. But Gladys didn't take a blind bit of notice as she sipped her cuppa and talked like an express train.

'Well, I'll bring you a few, then, Theresa, shall I?' she said kindly. 'When you've read them you can take them down the stall on Watford market that sells them second-hand and get some new ones. Just write your initials on the inside flap of the ones you've read because all the covers look the same, don't they? It's the only way I can keep track of all those sheikhs, doctors and the like!'

Despite my mother's misgivings, though, I liked my father's pigeon friends. There was just one I wasn't so sure about.

'Fancy a game of Scrabble, Mary?' he'd said one afternoon, as we sat in the living room.

Half an hour later, we were alone when the man handed me the bag containing all the Scrabble letters.

'Put that on your lap, will you, love?'

With no hint of an expression on his face, he plunged his hand into the letter bag and started furiously rummaging around.

'Hope I get an A,' he said, as he pulled out a tile and looked at it. 'No. Ah, well. Let's get another, shall we?'

He had six more tiles to get and picking each one seemed to take a strangely long time.

I never played Scrabble with him again.

Anne French cleansing milk

I sigh as I inspect my face in the mirror. There are bread-crumbs stuck all over it. Ripping off a bit of cotton wool and pouring cleanser onto it, I start to scrub. If the bright orange nylon overall that I have to wear at Garner's each week isn't bad enough, then removing all the breadcrumbs impacted on my face by the end of each day is. I didn't realize that working would have downsides like this. But it's worth it for the brown envelope I get at five o'clock each Saturday night. I'm saving up for a pair of Kicker boots and it won't be long now until I can afford them.

Geraldine Quinn, Lorraine Attard and I had all started work after turning fifteen. Geraldine had got a job in the green-grocer's, which I decided would be too cold, and I wouldn't be seen dead working as a Saturday girl in a North Watford hair salon, like Lorraine, because it was way too naff. I'd learned a thing or two about hair since Joe started training as a stylist after a year working on building sites.

Dad had spotted the advert in the *Watford Observer* asking for young creative people to apply for a junior position in a swanky salon in Stanmore.

'It will be perfect for you,' said Mum, as she packed Joe off for an interview. 'You tell them that you got your art A level at fifteen. Take your certificate and show them your book of bird drawings too. They won't find more creative than you. You'll not go anywhere in life if you stay on that building site.'

Joe had got the job and immediately started to thrive as he discovered an innate talent for hair-styling. You could almost hear Mum's sigh of relief when he came back each evening and told her what he'd learned that day as they sat together at the kitchen table. Suddenly Joe was happy again, the clouds that had hung over him for the past few years lifted. He loved the work and Mum didn't blink an eye when he gave me the latest cut dyed a fetching purple. Rules had to be followed when it came to behaviour and school, but fashion, music and art were never censored.

'I like to see you all dressed up,' she'd say, as we appeared in the kitchen. 'Although I'm not so sure about those, Mary.'

I'd just bought a pair of 1950s-style cream granny sandals

from a dance shop in Rickmansworth. 'But it's the latest fashion, Mum,' I cried.

'Well, be that as it may, they look like something my mother would have worn.'

I spent my Saturdays at Garner's behind the counter serving customers alongside the manageress, Mrs Tanner, while Ethel – who looked like a rubber doll and must have been almost seventy – stood out the back furiously slathering slices of bread with butter before filling them with egg and salad cream or cheese and pickle.

'I'll have one bloomer, three split tins, and how much is the custard slice, love?' customers would ask, as they stood three deep at the counter. 'And give us four apple turnovers and three doughnuts, too.'

Desperately trying to add it all up in my head, I lost count most of the time. But Mrs Tanner didn't correct me too often as I went to the till and pulled down the levers to ring everything up, so I guessed I wasn't too far wrong.

Each lunch break, I'd meet up with Geraldine and Lorraine to go and flick through the records in Woolworths. Or we'd go into Boots to see Tish and her friend Angela Horne before spraying ourselves with Charlie and Tweed. Blasé was my favourite and I couldn't wait to buy a bottle.

The best bit of my working day, though, was the moment when I was given an iced apple doughnut for my mid-afternoon break: I'd decided I needed to put on weight. Flares and skinny rib jumpers might have been perfect for my straight-up-straight-down figure, and there had been more kisses after Stephen Bradley, but I still envied Tish's looks. I had fried eggs, she had proper boobs. I had dead straight hair whereas hers was thick, falling in luxurious copper waves to her shoulders.

'How much does it cost to get to America?' I had asked Mum one day, as I flicked through a magazine.

'No idea,' she replied. 'But why do you want to go to America?'

I looked up at her. 'I'm too skinny, and however much I eat it doesn't seem to make a difference.'

'And what does America have to do with that?'

'Well, they eat loads there.'

'Do they?'

'Yes.'

She started to laugh. 'Ach! Get away with you! You're perfect as you are.'

I looked at her seriously. 'I need to go, Mum. I really do. It's easy to put on weight there.'

She bent down to give me a kiss. 'Mary Newton,' she said, as she smiled. 'What are we going to do with you?'

'But, Mum!' I persisted. 'I've got to go.'

'But why? Why do you have to go?'

'Isn't it obvious?' I sighed, as I rolled my eyes. 'Marc Bolan got fat there.'

Pernod and black

My stomach lurches slightly as I stand at the bar. Tish has brought me to the New Penny and it's the first time I've been to a nightclub.

'You'll keep an eye on her, won't you?' Mum had said to Tish, as we came downstairs earlier. 'Don't forget she's only fifteen and can sniff out trouble like a bloodhound.'

'I know, Mum, but we'll be fine. I'll make sure she's okay.'

My mother looked at me. I'd borrowed Tish's grey high-waisted peg trousers and put them on with a white shirt Katharine Hepburn-style and a pair of platforms. Joe had cut my hair into a short page-boy style and I'd slathered myself in Mum deodorant because I'd seen Tish do it religiously before a night out.

'Go on, then,' she said, with a smile, then kissing us both. 'Have a nice time and do what your sister says, won't you?'

'Course, Mum.'

We'd met up in the New Penny car park with Susan Durkin and Angela Horne, who'd opened her massive clutch bag to reveal a bottle of Liebfraumilch. After quickly downing it, we walked inside but I had no idea what to order when we got to the bar.

'I'll have a Pernod and black,' Angela said.

'Me too,' I replied quickly.

My first experiments with alcohol had taught me that everyone seemed to add blackcurrant to whatever they drank and I understood why as I gulped down the Pernod. It tasted like medicine but I forced it down.

Two drinks later and I can feel the Liebfraumilch bubbling in my stomach. I stagger to the loo. Staring into the mirror, I see two little blackcurrant horns on either side of my mouth. My head feels light as I have a pee and walk out to wash my hands. I wouldn't mind another drink but haven't got any money left, and Tish won't buy me one because she'll say I've had enough.

A glass has been left on the side of the sink. After looking left and right, I knock its contents back. And I immediately start to gag. Running back into the club, I find Tish in the middle of the New Penny dance-floor.

'Tiiiiiiiiish!' I scream, trying to make myself heard above the music. 'Tiiiiiiiiiish!'

'What is it?' she shouts, and I lean towards her.

'I've just drunk piss.'

'What?'

'I'VE JUST DRUNK PISS.'

Retching and gasping for air, I think of the urine that's now mixing with Pernod and Liebfraumilch inside me.

'Don't you dare be sick in here!' Tish says fiercely, and drags me outside.

I reel around the pavement as people stare and my sister looks at me furiously. 'How on earth did you end up drinking THAT?' she yells.

'It was in the loo. I thought it was brandy or something.'

'And since when do you drink brandy?' Tish hisses. 'Look at the state of you! How am I going to get you home? Angela's dad was supposed to be picking us all up.'

She drags me down Market Street and into Lucketts cab office.

'Is she drunk?' the controller says, as he sits eating a kebab.

'AM I DRUNK?' I roar, as I stagger around on my platforms.

'Get 'er aut of 'ere,' the controller replies.

We stand in the road where I am promptly sick. It takes half an hour for Tish to convince the taxi controller that I am well enough to travel in one of his cars.

'This is going to cost me a quid,' she says. 'You are going to pay me back every penny, Mary!'

When we reach home, the world is still whirling. We find Michael in the kitchen. He takes one look at me and tears a strip off Tish. 'You were supposed to be looking after her!'

'It's not my fault. You know what she's like! I'm going to watch telly.'

Tish slams out of the kitchen as my brother gazes at me. 'Let's get you to bed, shall we?'

Lying down, teeth cleaned and face wiped by Michael, I taste Pernod scratching at the back of my throat as the room reels around me. I swear that I will never drink again.

Bird's Eye Super Mousse

I stare out of the window for the hundredth time. It's 8.55 p.m. and Chris Miles is nearly an hour late. But however many times I stare down Windsor Road, I don't see him.

Embarrassment burns through me. Chris has a motorbike and wears a white suit. He's a bit naff but I really thought he liked me.

Dad's watching TV in the Front Room and doesn't know I'm going on a date. I'd never dare tell him. But Mum will help sneak me out of the house, like she always does.

'How about a mousse?' she says, as she walks into the Front Room.

'*Muuuuum!* I'm not a baby any more!'

'I know. But if you're sitting here waiting you might as well have something nice to eat.'

Every problem can be solved by food, as far as my mother is concerned. If I cry, she gives me slivers of meat off a joint; if I am disappointed, she cuts me a slice of cake. Without a word she leaves the room and returns with a mousse and a spoon for me. I open it silently, digging in the spoon and feeling hot tears of rage prick behind my eyes.

'It's his loss,' Mum says quietly, as she sits down beside me.

'But it's so embarrassing! Everyone at school knows we're going out. What will I say to them?'

'You tell them the truth and keep your head high. It's not your fault he's an eejit wit no morals.'

'But he isn't!'

'Well, he is if he leaves you sitting here. You're a lovely girl and he should be proud to have you on his arm. But trust me when I say that it won't seem so bad in the morning.'

'Really?'

'Yes, really.' She puts her hand over mine and squeezes it. 'Now don't you be worrying yourself over that fella. There'll be plenty more where that Chris-no-morals-eejit came from.'

I dig out the last bit of the mousse.

'Come on, now,' Mum says. '*Poldark*'s about to start.' She leans over to kiss me. 'And have another mousse, why don't you?'

Careers advice

'Teaching maybe?' Sister Angela says. 'Oh, no. That won't do at all, now, will it?'

I'm sitting in a careers advice interview with a nun who has only ever worked for God. My O levels are coming up and I have to pick my A levels for next year.

'So what do you want to study in the sixth form?' Sister Angela asks.

'Art, sociology and English.'

I'm still banned from Miss Stephenson's class but apparently she's going to be joined by another teacher next year who, I hope, will let me do my A level. There's also a wonderful new English teacher called Miss Coleman, who gets us to recite poetry, and while everyone else mumbles it at the front of the class, I dress up in costume or theme my recitation. Never knowingly underperformed.

'I was thinking of nursing, maybe, but those subjects won't do for that,' Sister Angela says, in her soft Irish lilt, as she looks at me quizzically. 'How about the secretarial course?'

I look at her in horror. Secretarial sixth is run by Mrs Duncan, and girls sit in lines tapping out letters on their typewriters, like Stepford Wives.

'I don't want to be a secretary!' I yelp.

'So just what is it that you'd like to do, Mary?'

I know exactly. I want to go to drama school. Mr Harold thinks I could get in but he only runs the drama club in his spare time so he has no idea how you actually get a place at the Royal Academy of Dramatic Art or the London Academy of Music and Dramatic Art. Sister Angela is my only hope.

'I want to study drama,' I say.

'Draaaaama?' she exclaims 'What draaaaama?'

'Acting, the theatre. I want to go to drama school.'

'But don't you cause enough drama as it is, Mary? Do you really want more?'

I look Sister Angela straight in the eye. 'Yes, I do. I want to be an actress.'

'An actress?'

'Yes.'

'You mean go on the stage?' Sister Angela squeaks, as the light finally dawns.

'Yes.'

As I watch her face turn the colour of a tomato, I realize that I might as well have told Sister Angela that I want to be a prostitute. My acting ambitions are never mentioned again at school.

Bell's whisky

'Jesus wept and Mary cried!' my mother shrieks. 'Go and get your father, boys! GO AND GET YOUR FATHER!'

Mum is in the Front Room staring down the road. My father is staggering up it.

'For the love of God, get him into this house!' Mum yells, as Joe and Lawrence stare open-mouthed at Dad.

Three hours ago my father left for the pub with Jack Davis. Given that he drank perhaps one whisky a year and never went to the pub, it was a memorable occasion. But yesterday one of Dad's birds won the Thurso race – one of the biggest there is – and it's the custom for the winner to stand drinks for the club.

'I'll have the roast on the table at two,' Mum had said, as we waved them off.

Dad's victory was all the sweeter because he'd snatched it from the jaws of possible defeat. While he was anxiously waiting for the pigeons to come back, he'd had to nip out to an emergency at Clements and told Lawrence to wait in the back garden for the pigeons until he returned.

'But, Dad!' Lawrence moaned as Dad picked up his car keys.

Manchester United were playing Southampton in the Cup Final and my brother could not bear the thought of missing a minute.

'I'll be twenty minutes,' Dad said, as he gave Lawrence a stern look. 'Now, get out into that garden and make sure you don't miss a thing. You have to clock in the first bird the moment it arrives back. Any extra seconds could cost the race, do you understand me?'

Sunny-natured Lawrence looked as if he was about to have a stroke.

'Do you understand, Lawrence?'

'Yes, Dad.'

For at least half an hour, my brother had dutifully stood in the back garden – only nipping back in now and again to check on the game. But in the final nerve-racking minutes, as extra time loomed and neither team had scored, he stood transfixed in front of the television, forgetting all about the pigeons as he chewed his nails. Southampton powered the ball to the back of the net just before the referee blew the final whistle, my brothers' faces went white with horror and Dad walked back in just as Lawrence started to cry.

'What are you doing?' he roared. 'Why on earth are you inside? What about the birds?'

Running out into the garden, Dad found a pigeon sitting on the loft. 'Do you see?' he shrieked, grabbing the bird and shoving the tag around its ankle into his clock. 'Fecking Manchester United losing the cup won't be a patch on how sorry you'll feel if I lose this race.'

Huffing and puffing, Dad had headed off to the club to log his result only to return with his rage forgotten a few hours later. His bird had won.

'I'll just have a couple,' he had said to Mum, as he left with Jack for the pub.

A couple of dozen, more like. Lawrence and Joe shoot out of the house and run down the road. Bouncing off cars as he lurches from side to side, my father staggers into garden walls and trips off pavements. Then Father Bussey's car turns into the bottom of the street.

'Boys!' my mother screams, as she runs outside. 'Quick now! Quick. Quick. The priest is coming. For the love of God, get him inside!'

But my father is a big man and even heavier now he's full of drink. Lurching under his weight, my brothers drag him up the road as Father Bussey pulls up outside the Chassels' house. Getting out of the car, he stares at my mother, who is holding Dad by the scruff of his neck and heaving him up the front step.

White as a sheet, she drags him inside and slams the door. Dad reeks of whisky as he lurches over to the stairs and sits down, gazing up at her with bleary eyes. 'Theresa, my darling!' he says, with a smile.

'Don't Theresa me, Sam Newton!' she roars.

'But I won the race. Now come and give me a kiss!'

'A kiss? There'll be no kisses for you. The shame of it. Now get yourself upstairs and I'll bring you a cup of tea.'

With that, Mum marches back into the kitchen and wails. The Sunday joint was resting on the side and the dog has nicked it amid the chaos of his master's return. It will be weeks before the atmosphere fully thaws.

'Dancing Queen'

The heat is so intense it curls around us as we sleep and we wake up sweating. It shimmers on the beach as we lie on towels slathered in sun cream and hits us like a wall when we walk out of cafés. It is the summer of 1976.

I have finished my O levels – the last exam provoking as little worry as the first and all the ones in between – and spent weeks tanning my snow-white skin at Rickmansworth Aquadrome. Lying on a towel next to Carrie and Debbie, listening to a transistor playing 10cc's 'I'm Not In Love', I feel as if the future is finally starting. After years of watching my brothers and sisters spread their wings, I am finally going on my first proper holiday.

Mum had booked Tish, Sadie and Don's daughter Marie and me a room at a B-and-B in Weymouth.

'The landlady's called Newton!' Mum had said excitedly. 'She must be trustworthy.'

All Tish and I had to do was save our spending money, and I'd hardly touched any of the pay packets from my new job at Boots, where I earned more and could finally raid the cosmetics shelves with my staff discount.

I'd never known anything like that summer: fires breaking out in scorched forests, tarmac turning sticky underneath our feet and people queuing at standpipes to get water. Weymouth might as well have been Spain as we sat roasting on the beach before going for an ice cream or sausage, egg and chips in a café. The beach was packed with sunbathers who turned lobster red as the sun beat down. People lay in the shallows to cool down, dogs panted underneath sunshades and little old ladies eased sandals off feet swollen by the heat.

When the sun finally cooled a little, we'd head off to the funfair before visiting the pubs and clubs on the front. Joe had cut my hair into Joanna Lumley's Purdey style – bleached blonde with dark underneath – and my favourite outfit was a bright red jumpsuit from Miss Selfridge with 'Shell' written on it; I cinched it in with a belt saying 'Eveready'.

and Johnny Rotten 'shit'. My mother's face is going whiter by the second, as Joe, Lawrence and I hold our breath in anticipation of what will come next.

Bill's just chatted to a woman with bleached blonde hair who's with the group and suggested that they can meet after the show.

'Dirty bastard,' says Steve Jones. 'Dirty fucker.'

With a cry of disgust, my mother strides towards the television.

'Turn it off!' she shrieks. 'Turn it OFF!'

'But, *Muuuum!*'

In desperation, she pulls the socket out of the wall and the TV goes black.

'I will not have that filth in my house!' she yells, before storming off to the kitchen.

I look at my brothers and smile. The Sex Pistols are amazing.

BaByliss hot brush

Am I in love with Kate Jackson? I wonder, as I fold my hair into the BaByliss. And if I am, then does it mean I'm a Lebanese?

Steam rises as I pull the tongs, determined to get a flick into my dead straight hair.

The first woman I felt like this about was Kiki Dee. But there aren't many lesbians in Watford so I'm really not sure what one looks like. Besides, I've enjoyed my romances with Sean, Stephen, Neil and Ian. None of them was serious but I

liked the dates and kisses on the front seat of their cars until
Mum appeared on the porch at midnight to put out the milk
bottles. To avoid this, I now get my dates to drop me off down
the road. It had worked a treat until Paul Craddock asked me
to go for a drink when I was on a night out at the Artichoke
in Croxley Green.

Paul was nineteen, his dad played golf and his brother's
girlfriend looked like Julie Christie, all long blonde hair and
even longer tanned legs. I had to look my best on our date.
Going through Joe's wardrobe while he was out at work, I
spied a silver blue mohair cardigan that he'd just bought
from Lui, Watford's only designer boutique. Joe was doing so
well in hairdressing that he could afford all the best gear but
would never let me borrow any of it.

I couldn't wear the cardigan on the sly, though, because
Mum did all our washing and would spot it. So, instead of
putting it on, I hid it on the porch before we all sat down
for tea. Angela had come over before she and Tish went out.
Michael's friend, Mick, was also there and Joe had brought
home Kevin Gilmartin. It was always the same on Saturday
nights – all of us plus extra – digging into whatever Mum had
cooked before heading out to different places and meeting up
for last orders at the same pub.

Ten of us squeezed into the living room as Mum bustled
in and out with the dishes, and I necked my supper eagerly,
anticipating Paul's arrival in his Ford Cortina. At eight o'clock,
I retrieved the hidden cardigan from the porch after dousing
myself in Blasé and walked down the road to meet him.

Paul took me to the Boot in Sarratt where I finally relaxed, knowing we'd never bump into Joe. It was almost midnight when I walked back up the path to the house. None of us had a key because Mum always left the back door unlocked and a piece of paper on the kitchen table with our names listed on it. We had to cross off our own when we got in so she could check we were all safely home, and the last in locked up.

But as I walked into the back garden, I saw the light on. Joe must be home. He'd be having a cup of tea with Michael or something. I decided to hoist myself in through the Front Room window but, one leg in and one leg out, an old man walking up the street mistook me for a burglar and started shouting as I climbed through the window.

'Whatcha doin'?' he yelled. 'Breakin' in, are ya?'

'It's my house!' I called, before hurling the rest of myself inside and landing on the carpet.

As the man outside screamed that he was going to call the police, I looked up to see Joe staring at me. He'd been sitting on the sofa listening to music in the dark.

'You are a joke, Mary!' he snarled, as he spotted his cardigan. 'And who the hell is that nutter shouting outside?'

Joe made sure I didn't touch his wardrobe again, and after a few dates my romance with Paul Craddock fizzled out.

I sigh as I pull the tongs out of my hair and the tiny bit of flick I've managed to get into it immediately starts to drop. My hair is constantly frustrating me but boyfriends don't. I'm having too much fun to be sitting next to the same guy at the Odeon each weekend, eating popcorn and holding hands. And I don't really care if I'm a Lebanese or not either. All I am sure of, as I watch Kate Jackson high-kicking in her white flares on *Charlie's Angels*, is that she has the best hair on the planet.

Kerrygold butter 2

Boys arrived at St Joan's in my lower-sixth year when the grammar-school system changed. Suddenly there were Toms and Christophers running around, as well as a new headmaster called Mr Cartmell, who was going to do a year's handover with Sister St James. Testosterone was in the air and everything was different.

I'd chosen English, art and sociology as A levels but academics still didn't interest me much. The only thing I continued to really thrive at was performing under Mr Harold's guidance. Getting home after performances, I'd sit down with Mum at the kitchen table as I told her all about the plays.

I knew she was pleased I'd found something I loved but I still didn't dare tell my parents about my theatre ambitions. Mr Harold had found out about drama schools for me – the Central School of Speech and Drama, LAMDA and RADA – and I was determined to apply. But I wasn't sure how Mum and Dad would react. Dancing, music and acting were hobbies, not real jobs. Dad would probably hit the roof and Mum would worry that it wasn't steady enough. What kid from Watford became an actor?

Still, though, I threw everything into performing, and when we decided to raise money for charity I got all my classmates together to put on a pop show. After selling tickets, the whole of the school trooped in to see us. Stephanie Elsie came on as Alvin Stardust, while Debbie Hunt, Angela Walmsley and Heidi Ginger belted out the Three Degrees. Cathy Lipscombe danced across the stage as the leader of Pan's People, with Geraldine, Shirley, Margaret and Lorraine behind her, gyrating to Supertramp, and Margaret Woodhead got the unfortunate job of impersonating Noddy Holder. I dressed up as Jimmy Savile with a cigar in my hand. I'd spent hours watching him on *Top of the Pops* and was only too pleased to put on a tracksuit to impersonate the man who was then loved by millions.

The show was a massive success and, after realizing that I could unite my classmates in a shared cause, I decided to put myself up in the vote for next year's head girl. I wasn't the most obvious choice – not top of the class or the best behaved – but I'd proved that I could get people working together and the Queen had just celebrated her Silver Jubilee so I fancied being a bit of a leader too.

The vote was done a couple of weeks before the end of the summer term and I was soon called into Mr Cartmell's office.

'Hello, Mary,' he said, as I sat down in front of him.

Surely I must have won. As far as I knew I hadn't done anything wrong for at least a month.

'I don't know you very well yet because our paths haven't crossed,' Mr Cartmell said. 'But I wanted to let you know that you've been voted head girl.'

My face broke into a broad smile.

'You should be very proud that you've been chosen because

it means that you're liked and respected by your friends. It's a job they think you can do.'

Then he shifted nervously in his seat. 'But I'm afraid that we cannot act on this vote because some of the teachers feel that you are not responsible enough to hold the position of head girl,' he said.

'What do you mean? I won the vote. I got the job.'

'I know, Mary. But some members of staff do not think you are suitable for the job and have vetoed the vote. They will not agree to you becoming head girl. I'm very sorry.'

Without saying a word, I got up and left the office, pushing down my tears as I walked home. But they started to flow the moment I got inside the house and found Mum in the kitchen, buttering bread.

'What's happened?' she said, as I walked in and threw my bag onto the table.

'I was voted head girl but Mr Cartmell told me I can't do it,' I sobbed.

'Whatever do you mean?'

'He said that some of the teachers were against it. They don't think I'm suitable.'

Mum wrapped her arms around me as she covered my head in kisses. 'Oh, darling,' she said. 'I'm so sorry.' She held me close as she spoke in a quiet voice. 'More fool them. They don't know what they've missed.'

'Do you really think so?'

'Yes, I do. You might be a bit of a handful, Mary, but you've got a big heart.'

'Have I?'

'Yes. But the thing about life is that sometimes your face just doesn't fit and it's not a failing of yours but the people around you.' She chucked me tenderly under the chin. 'Now dry your tears.'

Mum got a plate out of the cupboard and put a couple of slices of bread on it. The butter was extra thick. 'That should cheer you up now,' she said, with a smile.

R White's lemonade 2

'Mum's in bed,' Michael said, as I walked into the house a few days later. 'But I can't get an appointment with the doctor until tomorrow.'

'What's wrong with her?'

'I don't know. She says it's her head but she's not making proper sense. The doctor is full tonight. He said to bring her down in the morning.'

'But Mum's never ill.'

'I know. That's why I want the doctor to see her.'

'Where's Dad?'

'Work. He said he'd be home by seven.'

Mum was lying on her bed as I walked in to see her. She looked pale and feverish, mumbling a string of almost silent words that I couldn't understand.

'Mum?' I said. 'Are you okay?'

She clutched at her temples.

'Is it a bad headache, Mum?' I asked. 'Why don't I go down

to the shop and get you some lemonade? Will that make you feel better?'

She stared at me, her eyes focusing on mine for a moment. 'What's lemonade?' she said.

'What do you mean, Mum? Lemonade! Lem-o-nade.'

Her eyes slid away from mine as she started to mutter again.

'Mum?' I said. 'You'd like a glass, wouldn't you? I'll walk down to the shop and buy a bottle. You love lemonade. It's your favourite.'

But she didn't reply. Instead she just kept muttering to herself and fear solidified like ice inside me as I looked at her.

Camel coat

The doctor's glasses are so thick they make his eyes look like frogspawn.

'How long has your mother been unwell?' he barks.

'Since yesterday. She says it's her head and her neck is aching too.'

Why did he make us come here? Mum has only ever called a doctor to our house once in all the years we've been in Watford. She'd never bother the GP for no good reason so why couldn't he just visit us at home?

Mum is wearing her best camel coat but her hair is sticking up in tufts. She'll be so angry when she knows I let her go out looking like this. The trouble is, this doctor doesn't know Mum because the GP who looked after us for years has retired and she hasn't met his replacement properly.

'Let me know what he says,' Dad had said, as he left for work earlier. 'It's a busy day and there's no one to cover me. Tell the doctor that she was pointing up at the ceiling last night. Nearly scared the life out of me. I can't get any sense out of her.'

What could it be? I'd wondered, as I helped Mum get dressed. Maybe she was delirious. I knew that one of Joe's friends had seen pink elephants climbing up the wall once when he was ill.

'So it's your head, is it, Mrs Newton?' the doctor says to Mum, as she sits quietly in front of him.

I wish he knew her, understood that she usually talks nineteen to the dozen, not the gobbledegook she's mumbling now.

'Make Joe pork chops,' she'd muttered, as I helped her get dressed. 'Make Joe pork chops.'

'Course I will.'

'Tish. Postcard. Postcard.'

'What do you mean, Mum? She'll send one but she's only been gone a few days. It will take a while to get here.'

Tish had gone on holiday to Spain with Marie the week before and I'd wished I was going with her as I watched her pack.

'It'll be your turn soon,' Mum had said to me, as she helped Tish, layering tissue paper between her clothes to make sure they weren't too creased. 'Next year you'll be eighteen and then we'll think about letting you loose on the Continent.'

With a frown on his face, the doctor listens to Mum's heart

and takes her temperature. Then he shines a light into her eyes and sits back down at his desk.

'I think your mother is going through the change,' he says, as he looks at Michael and me. 'Women can get a little down at times like this. Depressed and erratic. Do you understand what I mean?'

One of Mum's cousins suffered with her nerves. It had got so bad that she didn't even recognize her own family and had had to go to hospital. Does the doctor mean that this is what's happening to Mum? But she's never been up and down in her moods. She's always steady, always there.

'I'm going to give your mother a prescription for some anti-depressants,' the doctor tells us. 'I want you to take her home and make sure she doesn't stay in bed. It will do her no good to be hiding away. She needs to be up and out. Women can suffer when they are going through the menopause but you mustn't let her wallow in it.'

He looks at us. 'A couple of weeks or so and she'll be back to normal. Just make sure she takes her medication.'

His words ring in my head as we walk Mum back to the car. Two weeks. Just two weeks.

Milk of Magnesia

'The doctor knows what he's talking about,' Dad says, as he sits at the kitchen table. 'Your mother will be fine soon enough.'

'But she's getting worse,' Michael says. 'You didn't see her

133

this afternoon. I think we should take her back to see the doctor.'

'Well, it's too late tonight. Let's see how she is in the morning, shall we? She'll be upset if she thinks we made a fuss over nothing. You only saw the doctor yesterday.'

Dad gulps down a spoon of Milk of Magnesia and sighs. 'Now let me get on with this paperwork, will you? I've got to get it done tonight.'

I think of the day when I was about six and Eric Kettle brought Dad staggering home from work. His stomach ulcer had burst and he'd been taken straight into hospital.

'You're working too hard!' Mum had told him, as we sat by his bedside.

'Stop your worrying, Theresa,' Dad had replied. 'I'll be right again soon enough. I've got to earn a wage, now, haven't I?'

He was back at his desk within days.

'The doctor knows what he's doing,' Dad says to us. 'Let him do his job. You only saw him yesterday. Let the pills do their work.'

But if he had seen Mum earlier today then maybe he wouldn't be so sure. Michael and I had taken her for a walk just as the doctor had told us to but she was too weak to go far. We took her home and left her sitting in the Front Room while we went to make a cup of tea. But coming back, we found Mum crouching down behind the swivel chair, scratching at the fabric and mumbling.

I keep thinking about what we're going to tell her when she's better. Mum will be angry that we took her out when she wasn't herself. But we've got to do what the doctor says. I know her cousin got better after she went into hospital but I don't want Mum going somewhere with strangers. I want her here with us. We'll look after her and we won't tell her anything about how she's been when she gets better. We'll just say she wasn't quite herself for a few days.

'Will Mum be all right?' Lawrence had asked me, after Michael and I had got her back to bed.

Joe's just given him a great new haircut and at fourteen he's beginning to grow up. But suddenly Lawrence looked so small and frightened as he stood in front of me.

'Course she will!' I said. 'She's going to be fine.'

But I'm afraid, too. It's as if the horizon has tilted. I don't understand what is happening. Have we done this to Mum? Have all the years of looking after us tired her out?

I leave Dad doing his books and go upstairs. Mum is lying still and quiet, mumbling every now and again as I lie down on the bed next to her.

'"Hail Mary,"' I whisper, as I hug her. '"Full of grace. The Lord is with thee. Blessed art thou among women and blessed is the fruit of thy womb Jesus. Holy Mary. Mother of God. Pray for us sinners now and at the hour of our death. Amen. Hail Mary. Full of grace. The Lord . . ."'

Mum starts to say the words with me. Full sentences.

'"Hail Mary,"' she says. '"Full of grace."'

Her voice is clear. God is looking after her. I know He is. Mum is going to be fine. Together we whisper the words of the rosary as the last rays of light seep out of the summer night's sky.

But the next morning she is no better.

'I'm ringing for an ambulance,' Michael says. 'This isn't right. She's been like this for three days now and I'm not going back to that doctor.'

There were no blue lights or racing speeds when the ambulance arrived. Michael phoned Dad to tell him what was happening and got into his car to follow the ambulance while I climbed inside it with Mum. It was only when she was pushed into Casualty that the world turned upside down.

'What drugs has she had?' a young doctor yelled at me, as he looked at Mum. 'What drugs has she had? How long has she been like this?'

'Anti-depressants,' said Michael. 'I've got the box.'

The doctor looked at the ambulance men pushing the trolley.

'Get her into the examination room. NOW.'

And then she was gone.

A hospital room

We were sure that Mum would recover. She was in hospital and the doctors would make her well again. Even when they diagnosed her with meningitis, we didn't really understand what it meant. No one explained. No one sat us down to tell us how serious it could be. We'd never even heard of meningitis and were so convinced Mum would soon be fine that Michael left for a holiday he'd previously booked with friends a couple of days after she went into hospital.

'Don't worry,' I said to him. 'We're all here and Tish is home soon. Mum will be wondering what all the fuss was about by the time you get home.'

When Tish got back from Spain, she, too, returned to normal life. After leaving St Joan's and working as a dispenser at Boots for two years, she'd got a place on a nursing course at University College Hospital and was due to start within a couple of days. She was told she'd lose her place if she didn't. She had no choice. We were on the phone every day to the hospital. Joe, Dad and I went in to see Mum daily and all of us went at weekends. But even as she lay still and silent on her bed, it seemed that no one could answer our questions.

When a doctor told us that Mum had encephalitis as well as meningitis and might be brain-damaged, if she recovered consciousness, I watched my father's spirit ebb away with each word. When she contracted pneumonia and was moved into intensive care, he sat by her bed for hour after hour and waited for her to wake up. We never stopped believing that she would because any other possibility was unimaginable.

No one explained just how misplaced our hope might be. The doctors had told us that Mum was seriously ill but also said that some people recovered from meningitis. These words were the only ones we clung to. We had no true understanding of what was happening and it was a time when patients and their families didn't question those in authority and medical information was scarce. Doctors walked away hurriedly from Mum's bedside before we got a chance to talk to them; nurses washed her and changed her sheets but didn't answer questions. Families were seen but not heard.

Dad didn't ask too many questions and we didn't either.

For eighteen days, we sat waiting for Mum to open her eyes as we prayed using the rosary we'd tied to the end of her bed. The slippers Tish had bought Mum as a present from Spain sat underneath her bed waiting for the day when she would be up again to wear them. It was as if we'd entered another world. Everything was grey, unfocused. We didn't know where we were or which direction we were heading in.

Robertson's raspberry jam

Mum looks thin. Like a tiny doll lying on the bed beside me. Even her hair looks different. Less red. The fire gone. I take her hand in mine. Her wedding ring is loose now. I should tell Dad. We don't want it to fall off.

I wonder what she'll want to eat when she wakes up. We'll have to make sure that she has exactly what she asks for. Maybe I can bake her a cake. A Victoria sponge. She likes those.

'Gentle, Mary!' she'd told me, the first time I'd made one with her. 'You've got to keep the air in the mixture so it will be light as a feather.'

She was standing beside me in the kitchen, patiently watching me cream together the butter and sugar in preparation for the flour and eggs.

'That's it,' she'd said, as she watched. 'You're doing well. Not too much, though.'

'But how do you know when it's enough?'

'You just know if you do it enough times,' she told me, with a smile. 'You'll learn. Now, what jam do you want to put in the middle?'

I looked at her.

'Well, I don't need to ask that, now, do I?' she said, as she reached into the cupboard and pulled out the raspberry jam.

I think of all the things that Mum knows how to do as I gently stroke her hand: how to get blackcurrant stains out of white shirts; how to knit a striped jumper; how to make lemon curd; how to sew the hem on a skirt. I've never asked her to teach me any of them because she is always there. I will, though, when she wakes up. Mum will show me. She always does.

Head tennis racquet

The phone rang early one evening soon after we got home from the hospital. I thought it would be Geraldine calling to ask if I wanted to play tennis. We hadn't told most people about Mum's illness, and as I looked at my racquet lying on the hall floor, I knew I didn't want to speak to Geraldine. What was happening felt so private that I couldn't find the words. I didn't want to speak them out loud.

But then I realized it might be the hospital. Mum might have woken up. Running to the phone, I snatched it up.

'Hello?'

'Is Mr Newton there, please?' a voice asked.

'No. This is his daughter.'

'Can you contact him?'

'Yes. But why?'

'This is Peace Memorial Hospital. We will need you to come down as soon as you can.'

I phoned Dad and Joe to ask them to meet us at the hospital before getting into the car with Michael and Lawrence. Tish's boyfriend, Phil, had gone to pick her up from the train and together we gathered in a room at the hospital. My heart clenched inside me as the doctor walked in. Not more bad news. Please don't tell us that she has got worse.

'I'm so sorry,' the doctor said, in a low voice, as he looked at us.

I stared at him, confused. What did he mean? I didn't understand.

'Mrs Newton passed away peacefully an hour ago,' the doctor said. 'Would you like to see her?'

My head feels light, as if I'm at the highest point on a swing, suspended in the moment when you feel weightless for a second before plunging downwards. I stare at the doctor. Mum can't have died. It isn't possible.

But then we walk into the room where she is lying still on a bed. My mother looks like one of the statues she's spent a lifetime praying to. As we wordlessly watch, Dad sits down on a chair beside her, stretches his body across hers and starts to sob.

Mushroom vol au vents

Mushroom vol au vents, egg sandwiches and Victoria sponge; pork pies, cheese on sticks and coffee cake; sausages, salmon rolls and iced buns. Don't forget three sugars for Aunty Peggy. Mustn't forget. Mum wouldn't want me to forget.

'Will you butter the bread, Tish?' I ask.

She looks like a wounded animal. So does Dad. When he put his arm around me at the funeral earlier, he felt smaller somehow. It's as if we've all been sent spinning in different directions and he's the furthest one away. When we got into the car a few days ago to go to the funeral director's, he had sat behind the wheel for a moment before his face crumpled and tears started to run down it.

'Please don't cry, Dad,' I said. 'Please don't.'

'But you've got all your lives ahead of you and I've got nothing,' he sobbed. 'She's gone. I've got nothing now.'

He wiped furiously at his face before starting the car, and we didn't say another word. But I knew in that moment that Dad couldn't be the one to keep us all going now. He was lost in his own grief. Michael was driving us forward but soon he'd be leaving because his job took him away a lot to places like Scotland and even Saudi Arabia. Tish was at college in London during the week and would only be back at weekends. It would be Joe, Lawrence, Dad and me from Monday to Friday, and Dad could hardly do a thing for himself, let alone us. A chasm had opened up in our family and I knew instinctively that I must stop everyone disappearing inside it. Mum would never have wanted us to fall apart without her.

'Has the kettle boiled?' Michael says, as he walks into the kitchen.

The house is full – people chatting, laughing as they remember Mum, crying sometimes too. Peggy, Betty and Agnes have come over from Ireland. Uncle Jim and Aunty Mary are putting some of them up in Camden and others are staying with us. Dick Froome is here. Bill Green too. Cathy, Jean and Ruth and their husbands. Irish Catholic friends from St Helen's, English ones from Watford, Father Bussey and Father John. I never knew Mum had so many friends until I walked into the church and saw that it was packed.

I'm relieved that the house is filled with people and chatter. There are people in and out all the time now, friends and relatives who bring us food and reminisce about Mum: talk about her, shed a tear or laugh as they remember. The house hums to the sound of Irish voices, the glug of the teapot being filled and women who gather me up in their arms. It's as if Mum is still here with us somehow. The presence of all these people distracts me from looking at her empty chair and the books beside it. These guests fill the house and paper over the gaping silence that I know will soon come.

Everyone will have to leave. They will go back to their own lives, their own families. I cannot imagine how we are ever going to learn to be six instead of seven.

Jonelle wash bag

I stare at the wash bag sitting on my bedside table. Mum gave it to me for my seventeenth birthday a couple of months ago.

'It's for when you travel,' she'd said, with a smile.

She knew I wanted to go abroad and see life, understood that I was ready to start spreading my wings just a little beyond the world she'd made for me. But now it's as if the guy ropes that have always tethered me to the earth have been cut and I'm floating.

I do not want to try to fly alone. Not yet. I don't feel safe.

Lamb with leeks

We sit silently at the kitchen table. We can't use the one in the living room yet. Not without her. We move around the house almost apologetically, not knowing how to fill it properly.

'Come on, everyone,' Michael says, as he puts plates in front of us. 'Eat up now!'

Everyone looks silently at their food. Mum would never have made lamb with leeks. Nor would she have bought potted shrimps and pâté. Michael is doing his best to look after us all but Lawrence and Joe seem lost and Tish cannot stop crying. I want to scream at her.

'Why don't we go up to see Mum today?' I ask her

sometimes, because I like to go to the grave and sit beside it, talking to Mum.

I tell her how I feel and how much I love her. Then I close my eyes as tight as I can and wait until I hear her voice inside my head and feel her with me. Nothing is real now except the grave and the fear in my stomach that sinks into place each morning in the first split seconds after I wake and the silence settles heavily on me. It is like a lead weight as I lie in bed willing myself to get up and go downstairs to the empty kitchen. No smell of toast or sound of the teapot being filled. No radio playing. Just emptiness. Our home is hollow. And however hard I try to fill it, I cannot.

Sometimes I find myself saying the words in my head.

'Mum is gone. Mum is gone. Mum is gone.'

But, try as I might, it feels as if someone else is speaking a language inside me that I do not understand.

Tish always shakes her head when I suggest going to see Mum.

'I just can't, Mary,' she whispers, and anger fills me.

We limp on through the summer, clinging together, turning in on ourselves as we shut out the world. Each night we sit in the Front Room talking about Mum, remembering her, not daring to stop talking for fear of losing her presence. The television doesn't go on. It would seem too normal to watch it. We cannot use the living room because Mum's chair is still there. By September, Tish and Michael have started work again. Six becomes four and I am left with Dad, Joe and Lawrence.

Condolences

'Ach, she was a saint your mother and no doubt about it,' the elderly Irish woman says, as we stand in the street. 'To think that she was right as rain one day and then gone. It's past thinking about. A woman like that. Five children too. She was a saint so she was.'

I stare at the woman, trying to get away, but she won't stop talking.

'I just couldn't believe it when I heard the news. "Not Theresa Newton," I said. It's a terrible thing. And her only a young woman. Tragic. Just tragic.'

Death, like birth, is a universal truth. But where one is celebrated, it felt to me that the other was often met with either too much talking or painful silence. I understood why my classmates didn't say much when I got back to school after the summer holidays. They simply gathered me up, carried me with them and I was thankful that they were there each day. School was something to cling to.

The only person at St Joan's who really talked to me about what had happened was Sister St James, who still came back occasionally and called me in to see her when the autumn term of my final A-level year started.

'I'm so terribly sorry about your mother, Mary,' she said gently. 'When you're a nun, people often think that you have made the greatest sacrifice by giving your life to God. But the most important thing anyone can do is to bring children into the world and raise a family. Your mother brought up five so that means she did the biggest job anyone can.'

A tear had slipped down Sister St James's face as she looked at me and I'd stared wordlessly back at her.

There were other people who reached out, too. Aunty Cathy, Ruth, Jean, Don, Sadie, Harry and Sheila dropped in whenever they could, arriving with meals and cakes as they bustled around making pots of tea and asking how we were or trying to get Dad to talk. But there were times when I almost wished they wouldn't come, moments when I saw grief etched so sharply on their faces that I wasn't sure I could face dealing with their loss as well as ours. I didn't want them to see us struggling, to know how hard we were finding it to cope.

My Boots supervisor, Jenny Xeri, would walk out of the shop to give me a hug when she saw me get off the bus from school, and one day her sister Bet came out with her.

'There isn't a God,' she'd said, as she stood with us. 'Because if there was, then how could He have let this happen?'

As I looked at her, I thought of Mum saying the Hail Mary as she was dying.

'There is,' I said, because I knew that He had been with her even as she was leaving us.

I understood why people used words like 'tragedy', 'devastating' and 'senseless' when they talked to me. But there was only one thing I wanted from them – hope – and no one could give it to me.

Atrixo hand cream

When I was a child, Mum would finish the washing-up and dry her hands before reaching for the tube of Atrixo she kept by the sink next to the Fairy Liquid. With a look of pleasure crossing her face, she'd rub it into skin worked hard by constant washing, cooking and cleaning. When I was sitting next to her at the kitchen table, the distinctive smell of Atrixo would fill the air as she asked me how I was getting on with my homework or what had happened that day at school.

Now I stare at the tube of cream still lying by the sink. Beside it is another one that Mum cut down to get the last bits out before throwing it away. Always careful. Always making the pennies last.

Each day I pick up the tubes and carry them to the bin. But every time I take the lid off, my hand hovers for a moment in mid-air before I turn and walk back to the sink. Then I carefully put the tubes back in the same place they've always been.

Glade air freshener

My heart thrums as I put my key into the lock. I still can't get used to having one. There never was the need before because Mum was always at home. I hate this key.

Cold cigarette smoke hangs in the air as I walk into the

house. Dad had a bad night last night and spent all evening alone in the Front Room listening to Josef Locke records. He does this every night now. He's even stopped feeding the pigeons so I have to do it. Dad just works, comes home and goes into the Front Room. It's almost beginning to feel like a relief when he does, though. At least Lawrence and I can then sit quietly together and watch television.

'Dad's just really sad,' I say to him, as we sit side by side. 'He'll get better.'

But I know that Lawrence won't sleep for hours to come when he goes up to his bedroom while I stay downstairs putting off the time until I, too, will have to go to bed. Doing some vacuuming or putting a wash on, I don't bother to think about the essays I have to write for school as the sounds of the music we once all listened to together play for my father alone in the Front Room.

It was only after my mother's death that I started to understand why she'd stuck to such a rigid routine all her life. My father was not a lazy man. With Mum gone, he would try to iron his shirts in the mornings and change the bed sheets with me at weekends. He did what he could, and Michael, Joe and Tish helped too at weekends. But Dad had no real clue about how to run a house so I had to learn.

My life divided into two distinct parts: the weekend when we were all at home together and the weekdays when it felt as if just Lawrence and I were living in the house because Dad was either at Clements or shut in the Front Room and Joe was always working.

With the start of the new school term at St Joan's, I quickly realized that I had to decide what jobs to do, and when, if I was going to stand a hope of keeping the house the least bit together. But I vacuumed one day only to find the carpets covered with muck the next, washed clothes but forgot to iron them in time for school and constantly ran out of bread and milk. Looking out of the window as I did the dishes, I'd see weeds growing in the garden. Our home was decaying around us.

I only realized that I had to change the sheets more regularly when they started to smell. The washing piled up and the ironing basket was constantly full. One day, as Lawrence left for school, I'd noticed that the collar of his shirt was dirty and had hardly been able to breathe when I saw it. I'd thought that heaping Omo into the washing-machine would be enough to get out the stains but it wasn't. Mum would never have let Lawrence leave for school like that.

Now I flick on the hall light before walking around the house and turning on all the rest. I switch on the television and the radio, anything to get rid of the dense silence that fills our home now. Opening a window in the Front Room, I pick up Dad's ashtray and walk back to the kitchen, where I reach into the cupboard underneath the sink and pull out a bottle of Glade. The smell makes me feel sick but I go back to the Front Room and spray it around. Anything is better than the stale smell.

It was always the same whenever I returned to our empty house at the end of a school day. I just wanted to keep my mind busy – reciting lines from plays or singing the theme tunes to adverts as I started peeling potatoes for tea. The words and lyrics would roll around in my head as the TV and radio played and I tried to stop myself letting my mind drift back. I was the centre now, the one who had to hold everything together for my father, Joe and Lawrence. Keep going. Just keep going. All I had to do was pull everyone along with me. Force them to continue.

But the heartbeat of our house had died with Mum and at first I'd tried to fill the space around my father and brothers with my noise, smiles and chatter.

'Sister Gabrielle had us in stitches today,' I'd babble, while we ate tea together. 'Cindy asked for a book from the top shelf in the library and we knew what was coming. We couldn't stop laughing when she clambered up the steps and we saw her tiny little bird ankles wrapped in these massive fluffy socks. But she got really angry and threatened to report us to Mr Cartmell.'

I soon saw that it was pointless. There was only one thing I could do: create a routine that would make my father and brothers put one foot in front of the other every morning. So, I'd get up at seven to lay up the breakfast table before cooking Dad his eggs and pouring Lawrence his cereal. I'd always try to make sure he ate something because Mum wouldn't want him going to school with an empty stomach. But Lawrence hardly ate and neither did I. Soon I had to start borrowing his trousers because mine were too big.

As I peel potatoes, I hear the key in the lock. I am sure Lawrence waits for me to get back each day because he doesn't want to come into an empty house.

'Hello,' I say, as he walks into the kitchen. 'Was school okay?'

'Yeah.'

Lawrence looks around, as if searching for something, before silently leaving the kitchen.

I stare into the sink as I think of Joe. He got back late last night: the house was in darkness when I heard the front door open. But as I waited for the creak that would tell me he was coming up the stairs, I'd heard a different sound – a cry so keen it sounded like a wounded animal's. I'd lain still in bed as I listened to my brother's heart breaking.

Dettol

Patch died on my thirteenth birthday and Mum missed him so much that we got a new dog about a year later. Sam was an older adult dog that needed a new home, a Greyhound Labrador cross with a strawberry gold coat. With hair the same colour as Mum's, he'd sit in front of the window and we'd tease her that the neighbours would think he was her. When she went out into the garden to call him, we'd joke that they'd think she was a fishwife calling her errant husband because Dad and the dog shared the same name.

We all loved Sam because he'd co-operate with any game: leaping over the jump courses that Lawrence and I made for him in the back garden or dancing on his hind legs as we dangled a biscuit from Michael's fishing rod. He was just as popular with other people too. When Sam was hit by a car and the vet realized my parents couldn't afford the bills, he came round in the evening to treat him for free. The dog and Mum's baking were a combination that was too hard to resist.

The person who loved Sam most, though, was Mum. For her, he could do no wrong. He was her constant companion.

'How's about an eggy for Sammy?' Mum would cry in the mornings, as she gave us breakfast.

Sam would look up at her adoringly as she fried him an egg before popping it into his bowl. After gobbling it up, he'd walk to where Mum had sat down at the table, then rest his head on her knee.

'Sammy, Sammy Soo,' my mother would croon, as she stroked him.

Now he sits with his head on my knee. We're at the vet's. I want to push Sam away. I wish he'd stop staring up at me with his brown eyes. I turn my head but can't stop myself reaching out my hand to him. His coat is so soft and thick, his skin warm beneath it.

Dad told me that I had to bring Sam here. Ever since Mum's death, the dog has been messing in the house because he's left inside all day. Sam is used to running in and out of the garden but suddenly he has to sit in the kitchen for hours on end and I often get home to find dog mess everywhere. I always clear it up and wash down the floor with Dettol before opening the windows. But I can't hide Sam's misdemeanours from Dad because the telltale smell of antiseptic always gives us away.

'I've had enough of it,' he'd told me a couple of days ago. 'You've got to take him to the vet. It's got to stop.'

Tears start to roll down my face as I sit with Sam. He can't help it. He's as lost as we are. I brush my tears away, embarrassed to be crying in public. But I can't stop them as I watch other people walk out of the consulting room with reassured smiles on their faces. The vet has told them that their pet will be well, no longer in pain or distress.

But I am not going to ask the vet to give Sam a pill or a vaccination. He will not hand me a cream to rub on him or a bottle of drops to put into his food tonight. Instead I must go into the consulting room and tell the vet that my father wants the dog put down.

'We just can't cope with him any more,' Dad had told me. 'It's too much. He's too old for a new home and it wouldn't be fair anyway to send him to strangers. He misses your mother too much. It's kinder like this.'

The weight of Sam's head on my knee feels like lead. I dig my fingers deeper into his coat, fighting the urge to run out of the waiting room. All I want is for Dad to stop being so sad.

Mother's Pride

I reach into the supermarket chiller, taking a quick look around me before bending down to the plastic packet of chops. Pulling at the price label, I peel it off, not daring to breathe as I stick it onto a bigger packet. I don't have enough money for chops that will feed us all. Dad leaves me cash on the kitchen table when he goes to work in the mornings but often it's not enough to buy what I need. I try to tell him but he just looks at me blankly.

'Your mother always made do,' he says gruffly.

Saying a silent Hail Mary, I pull the chops out of the chiller and look around me. No one has seen. I'm safe this time. But if it wasn't for the shopkeepers Mum visited for years, I'd never keep us going. Most days, I get off the school bus, go to see them and find they've put something aside for me.

'Your mum always liked lamb's liver,' the butcher says, as he hands me a packet. 'I've put a bit extra in. Just give me what you've got.'

Or I go into Dick Froome's and he hands me a box packed with all the basics that Mum used to buy each week: Omo, Kerrygold butter, Bisto, Oxo cubes, Robertson's jam and Homepride flour. Fishing the flour out of the box because baking is now a thing of the past, I replace it with a loaf of Mother's Pride as Mum's words about 'processed rubbish' ring in my ears. Then I walk around to Bill Green's shop, knowing I will find a box of vegetables left at the back door, if he's already closed, with a handwritten note telling me how to steam, roast or boil them. These men and their endless kindnesses to me are often all that keep me rooted in a day.

I have to leave school early now in order to get back in time for the shops or start cooking tea. There's no time for hanging about in the common room listening to the radio any more, and I can't do much drama because Lawrence has to let himself into the house if I stay late for rehearsals, which I don't like him to do too often. Mr Harold and Miss Coleman have helped me apply to RADA but I can't really think of what it might mean. The future doesn't seem real now. It's all I can do to get through each day so I scramble out of the door as soon as the final bell goes, knowing that Dad will want to eat the moment he gets in.

Try as I might, though, I can never cook things right. I take Mum's Marguerite Patten *Cookery in Colour* recipe book off the shelf and flick through it, follow the instructions to the letter, and it still doesn't taste right. Or I try to remember what I saw Mum do a thousand times and make one of Dad's favourites. Last week, I made mince with cabbage and potatoes but knew as I stirred the pan that I was doing something wrong. The mince was a dull grey colour. It smelt grey too.

'I can't eat this,' Dad said, after he'd taken a mouthful.

Then he got up, pushed his chair back and left the kitchen without a word.

'Boogie Nights' by Heatwave

I'm standing in the New Penny. Joe, Tish and Phil wanted me to come out.

'Come on, Mary!' Joe had exclaimed. 'It'll do you good. I'll look after you.'

It's a few days after Christmas. We sat like waxwork dolls as we tried to get through the day, all of us sighing with relief when it was over and we didn't have to pretend any more. We tried to keep Lawrence occupied and I think he enjoyed it. It's hard to know what he's feeling, though, these days. Lawrence has just turned fifteen and we bought him a skateboard from Alpine Sports. He seemed to like it. I hope he did.

Everyone around me is dancing as 'Boogie Nights' plays. My school friends are here, teenagers I know from Watford too. People come up to me to chat and ask how my Christmas was.

'Yeah, fine,' I say. 'We nearly burned the turkey but it came out all right in the end.'

I smile at them as I ask how their Christmas was, offer to get them a drink or pretend that I have to go to the loo, anything to get away. Everyone is dancing and smiling, throwing their heads back as they laugh at jokes. But as I stand in the middle of the dance-floor, I realize for the first time that I am no longer like everyone here. My friends are looking forward to celebrating the end of one year, hopeful about what the new one will bring. They are carefree but there is a weight inside me now. More and more, I cannot stop myself wondering if all the trouble I caused Mum somehow made her ill. She had so little. No holidays or meals out, new clothes or treats. She gave us whatever extra she had, and I ask myself if I wanted too much. The thought settles heavily inside me – expanding so quickly it makes me breathless. I was always giving Mum problems. Was it me who made her ill?

I will never know what I might have done better. She is never coming back.

'Mary?' I hear Joe say, as he puts his arms around me, and I feel tears wet on my face. 'Come on, Sis. Let me take you home.'

'Baker Street' by Gerry Rafferty

The radio is on as Lawrence and I stand peeling potatoes.

'I got my report today,' he says quietly.

I look at him. His face is white.

'It's really bad. I can't show Dad.'

'How bad?'

'I got Ds in maths, French and geography.'

I lean under the sink and pull out a saucepan. 'I'll sign it,' I say.

'You will?'

My heart twists as Lawrence looks at me.

'Of course,' I say. 'There's no point in Dad finding out. He doesn't have to know. Just make sure you do better next time, okay?'

Leg-warmers and Mary Janes

My stomach growls. I am standing in a large rehearsal room surrounded by about thirty other teenagers. I couldn't eat a thing when Tish met me earlier off the train to Euston and took me across to the canteen in her nursing digs at UCH.

'You've got to eat something,' she said, as I picked at some toast. 'You won't be able to think straight if you're hungry.'

But I was too nervous to eat and soon left her to walk across to Gower Street and through the doors of RADA for my final audition.

I'm wearing a pair of black Mary Janes, leg-warmers and drainpipe jeans. As people around me talk about audition pieces and what we're going to have to do, my stomach rolls with nerves. They have almost overwhelmed me each time I've come to RADA to perform. I've had two auditions so far and recited Shakespearean speeches, a scene from a Brendan Behan play and a speech from Arthur Miller's *A View from the Bridge*. I've cried, laughed and poured everything into each performance.

'Ladies and gentlemen,' a man cries above the noise. 'Welcome to you all and congratulations on getting this far. As you know, we get a lot of applications to study here and you've all done an excellent job in your auditions if you've made it to this final step of the process.

'We've seen all of you individually but today is about working with other actors. We want to see you perform alongside each other but remember that there's no right or wrong. We just want you to make the most of today and leave feeling as if you've got something out of it.

'Once we've seen you all, we'll be writing to offer successful candidates a place to study here. And, of course, letting those of you who haven't got places know so that you can take up offers you might have got from other drama schools.'

I wonder what Dad will say if I get offered a place. I still haven't talked to him much about RADA because I don't want to upset him any more than he is already.

'Why don't we take him out?' Don and Harry say, when they come over for tea.

'He's got to leave this house,' Sadie and Sheila whisper, when he wanders out of the room. 'It's no good for him being cooped up here. Theresa would hate to see him like this.'

This morning Dad was sitting at the kitchen table reading the paper as I got ready to leave.

'Where are you off to?'

'RADA. Final audition.'

He sighed as he turned the page. 'Why you want to be doing all that I just don't know. By your age I was out working. Not studying something that will surely never make you a proper wage.'

'But, Dad! People make a living by acting. Merry's dad has been in *Love Thy Neighbour* for years.'

'And no doubt putting ideas in your head.'

Merry Smethurst and her family have become one of the brightest spots in my life. Merry started at St Joan's in the lower sixth and lives in a house near Chorleywood Common. The Smethursts' garden rolls down a hill and Merry's mum, Julie, is always in it pruning roses or weeding, while her dad, Jack, sits in his cabin smoking cigars and reading scripts.

'You'll be fantastic on the stage, our Mary,' he says, when I go in to see him. 'Go and do it, get any job you can – sweep the stage, if you have to. It can be a hard life but it's a great one. And you've got the talent.'

As I sit with Jack, he tells me stories about his life as an actor. Sometimes I find other actors there whom I know from television when I go to stay for the night. But it's not them I want to see. It's Jack, Julie, Merry, Perdy, Jane and Adam. Their house is so full of life. It reminds me of how ours used to be.

Going over to see the Smethursts is sometimes all that gets me through a week.

'You need to get a proper job, Mary,' Dad said, as I put on my coat.

His words ring loudly in my head now as I look around the room.

'We're going to start with some warm-up exercises and movements,' the teacher says. 'So, first you will be warming up your voices and bodies by buzzing like bumble bees and working your arms.'

All around me people begin humming and buzzing, wriggling and looping their arms.

'Come on, now!' the teacher cries. 'Just let yourself go. This is the start of a big day for you all.'

But as people around me start to move, I'm not sure what to do. For the first time ever I feel embarrassed to perform.

Scotch eggs

I'm lying in the bedroom I still share with Tish. She's home for the weekend, and we're going out to the pub with Phil soon. Tish is on the bottom bunk, the one she's always slept in, and I'm on the top. Sometimes when she's at college during the week, I get into her bed just to feel closer to her. If Tish and Michael didn't come home each weekend, I'm not sure I could keep going. But I know as I wave them off each Monday morning that they'll be back on Friday. All I need to do is get through five days, four nights until they're home again.

'So what are you going to do if you get offered a place at RADA?' Tish says, as I lie above her reading *The Thorn Birds*.

'Dunno. I'm not sure how I'm even going to be able to afford it. My Boots money won't pay for it all and Dad won't give me any extra.'

I wish Tish would stop talking. Dad and money is an unsolvable problem.

'Your mother always made do,' he barks at me, when I tell him I've run out of housekeeping. 'I don't understand why you can't, too.'

The thing is, I'm only now beginning to discover just how many things Dad never really understood – not just how far Mum made so little money go. He's like a child almost, a weight on top of a weight, without her here to keep him going.

'Will you take the children into town, Sam, and give me a couple of hours' peace?' she'd say, on a Saturday morning.

'The fence needs a coat of paint.'

'Don't forget to change those light bulbs.'

'We need to get the bedding plants in. Will you nip to the nursery tomorrow?'

'I'm going out. Take the casserole out of the oven at six thirty and put the potatoes on. I'll be back in time to mash them.'

She was his compass and now he has lost direction. But while we all try to keep each other going, it sometimes feels that Dad is so lost in his own sadness that he doesn't think of ours. He just wants his life to continue as it did while Mum was here: meals on the table, shirts washed and ironed;

rooms polished and vacuumed. I don't mind filling the gap. I understand that I must be the one to look after my brothers and him. But money is the only thing I ask and it's a constant struggle.

Sometimes, if I'm really careful, I can scrape together enough to buy Lawrence or Joe a secret treat – a cake or a bun that I know they will like. Occasionally I keep enough back to buy myself something too: a massive Scotch egg.

'But what will you do if you don't go to drama school?' Tish asks.

'Dunno.'

'Mary! You're sitting your A levels soon. There's got to be something you want to do if you don't get a place. What about becoming a paramedic?'

'Are you joking, Tish? Can you imagine me in an overall rescuing people?'

'Maybe not.'

I turn a page.

'So what, then?' Tish asks.

'I don't know!'

Tish goes quiet and I stare at the ceiling. All the plans I was constantly making before Mum died have been forgotten. The future seems so far away now. As well as applying to RADA, I've been for an interview at Goldsmiths, University of London, to do an English degree but wasn't really sure why I was there as I sat answering the questions.

'Do you smell something weird?' Tish asks.

I bend over the bunk to see her scrabbling around the bed. 'What are you doing?'

'Trying to find whatever it is. There's such a bad smell in here. It's like something's rotting.'

'I can't smell anything.'

'Well, you must have a cold or something. It's disgusting whatever it is.'

Tish screeches as she burrows under her pillow. '*Mareeeeeeeee!*' she yells.

She holds up a Scotch egg covered with mould. It was tucked underneath her pillow. 'What on earth is this?'

I look at her and start to smile. 'Oh, shit!' I say. 'I must have forgotten it. I had to hide it from Dad. He'd only moan if he knew I'd spent ten pence on it. He's such a tight git. I swear I don't know how Mum ever put up with him.'

We look at each other and, without warning, after months of hush, our bedroom is suddenly filled again with the sound of laughter.

Aramis

'What does he think he looks like?' Tish cries, as she walks over to the buffet table.

We're standing in the working men's club where Dad's pigeon mates meet. Dad got a deal on hiring it for my eighteenth, and Tish and I did the buffet. The table is heaving with prawn cocktail vol au vents, cheese and pineapple on sticks, sausage rolls and Twiglets. For afters there are iced rings, Tunnocks tea cakes and a huge cake.

Michael looks confused, Joe is crying with laughter and a mixture of awe and hysteria flits across Lawrence's face as we watch Dad jive across the dance-floor. He is wearing brown flared trousers and a cream-and-brown striped shirt. His hair is slicked to his head with about three pots of Brylcreem. 'Night Fever' is playing. Our father suddenly can't get enough of disco.

'Get him off there!' I hiss at Joe.

'But look at the old man, Mary! He's having the time of his life.'

Jean and Ruth walk up to us with smiles covering their faces.

'You've done yourselves proud!' Ruth exclaims. 'What a party.'

'Make him stop!' I wail at her, as I point at Dad.

'Go on, Mary! He's having fun. It's good to see him smile at last.'

I know it is. It's just hard to keep up with the changes in him. One day Dad was sitting crying in the Front Room, the next he was like an excited teenager.

It had started when Phil told us about the Widows and Widowers Club in West Watford that his mum went to each Saturday night. 'Your dad should try it,' he'd said. 'My mum loves it.'

'That'd be perfect!' Tish cried. 'Dad used to like ballroom dancing when he was young, didn't he? It's been more than eight months. We've got to get him out of the house.'

Tish, Joe and I moved on him together when he was sitting watching *Rising Damp* one night.

'Come on, Dad!' we cajoled. 'It'll do you good.'

He grunted as he sat in front of the television.

'You never know, you might enjoy it,' we said.

He silently lit a Player's.

We often wondered if Dad realized just how like Rigsby he was.

In the end, we persuaded him to give the club a go and he arrived home so happy after one too many pale ales that he fell off his chair in the living room as he told us about the night.

'It was grand,' he said. 'Great music. Lots of people. Lovely to have a wee dance.'

We were delighted that he was having fun at last. We had no idea just how much, though, until we went to visit him in hospital following a long-awaited operation on his piles and found a very attractive woman called Bernadette sitting by his bed.

'What do you think he'll tell her he's had done?' I screeched with laughter, as we left. 'Do you think he'll take his rubber ring when they go for dinner?'

Bernadette didn't last long but my father didn't seem too worried. He suddenly had a new horizon and was going to make the most of it. Each Saturday night without fail, he got dressed in his best, slicked down his hair and headed off to see the other widows and widowers. It was good that he was enjoying himself again. I just wished he wasn't doing it quite so publicly because my new boyfriend was due to turn up any minute.

John. Mead. Just those two words were enough to make my stomach roll. As the younger sister of two brothers I had been in the constant slipstream of their friends – some I had dated, others I had admired from afar – but none had turned into a serious boyfriend.

I met John when he came round to our house for one of the haircuts Joe did for his mates after work. With chestnut brown hair and hazel eyes, he walked in wearing a tank top, jeans and brogues, looking like a cross between Jimmy Percy from Sham 69 and Christopher Blake from *Love for Lydia*. The next time he came over, I made sure I was ready.

'You're a bit dressed up for a Monday night, aren't you, Mary?' Joe had said, with a laugh, as I teetered into the kitchen.

John and I didn't talk much that night but I was determined to see him again and soon bumped into him at the New Penny where he asked me to dance to 'Wishing On A Star'. After that, I turned up week after week, hoping for another glimpse of him.

'What are you doing here again?' Joe would moan.

'Nothing!' I'd say, as I scanned the dance-floor. 'Now get us a drink, will you, Joe?'

But as much as I'd hoped John would phone me, I hadn't heard a thing until a couple of weeks before my birthday when Jenny Xeri had come to tell me that I had a phone call as I was working at Boots one Saturday. Racing to the staff room, I'd picked up the receiver.

'Mary?' I heard John say. 'I'm in a play tonight in Harrow. Would you like to come?'

One performance in, and I was convinced that we were destined to be the next Larry and Vivien after realizing that John loved drama as much as I did. After several nights out,

I now wake up each morning pining for the moment when I will see John again.

'He's here!' Tish hisses as we stand by the buffet table, and I look towards the door.

John's face breaks into a smile as I wave at him.

'Hello,' he says. 'Happy birthday! You look great.'

I'm wearing high-heeled clogs, a pale blue dress with a lace collar and a petticoat under the skirt. My hair has been cut into a plum-coloured crop. Joe decided I should go more punk but cut it too short. I cried for days but have taken to slathering myself with blue Rimmel eye shadow and pale pink lipstick to make up for it.

'Thanks,' I say breathlessly.

'This is for you.'

John hands me a present and I rip it open. *The Man-Machine* by Kraftwerk. It's another sign.

'Do you like it?' John asks.

'I love it,' I squeak.

The smell of Aramis fills the air as John bends down to kiss me. At last I understand what I've been listening to people sing about for years. I'm falling in love.

Angel Delight

I stare at the letter from RADA before shoving it into my satchel and closing the front door. The house is silent and Lawrence isn't in the living room. I walk upstairs to his bedroom. He's lying in bed. Still in the same place he was this morning when I left for school.

'How are you feeling?' I ask, as I sit down on his bed.

His face is pale and there are black shadows under his eyes. 'Okay,' he says.

'Did you sleep all day?'

'Yeah.'

'Feel like getting up now?'

'Dunno.'

'Come on,' I say. 'I'll go down and get tea on. Come and sit with me. I won't make you peel the spuds or anything.'

He gives me a weak smile and I walk back downstairs. Lawrence has a lot of days like this now, days when he is so exhausted he can't get out of bed after being up all night unable to sleep.

'Time to get up!' I say, on the mornings that he struggles. 'You're going to be late for school.'

Sometimes Joe and I manage to persuade him to get out of bed. But on other days we just can't bring ourselves to make him as he tells us it feels as if something is pressing on his chest.

'I can't breathe properly,' he says, when I sit down next to him. 'I can't get the air in.'

The more exhausted Lawrence gets, the worse his grades have become and now he dreads going into school. A few weeks ago, he brought home another letter from the head-master telling Dad that he'd got drunk at school. Once again, I forged Dad's signature and told him nothing about what had happened. He'd only shout and scream.

I put on the kettle, sit down at the kitchen table and get the letter out of my bag. After all this time and so many auditions, I've finally been offered a place at RADA. But I can't leave home to study and I'd hardly be here even if I carried on living in Watford and only went to London for lectures and rehearsals. I can't leave Lawrence. Not now. Mum didn't have a choice but I do and, besides, I need him as much as he needs me. Lawrence and I are a unit. Together we have created our own way of being. However flawed. We are home and we are together.

How would I pay for all the extras that college in London would cost anyway? I can't keep asking Michael, Joe and Tish for help. They already do enough for Lawrence and me – giving us money for clothes and going out, topping up my Boots wage and giving Lawrence a bit extra to the pay packet he gets for working as the car-park attendant at Clements.

I hate asking them. That's why I pulled a fast one in Freeman, Hardy & Willis a few weeks ago after buying a pair of display shoes that had been bleached by the sun and were being sold at a discount. I took them back a few days later when a different shop assistant was working and she exchanged them for a new pair. But if I can't even afford shoes, how am I going to pay for train tickets and meals, books and nights out?

Gulping down my tea, I hear my mother's voice in my head: 'You're scared, Mary Newton. And when were you ever scared in your life?'

But the thing is, Mum: I am. And I've felt this way almost every minute since you left. It's like the world went from Technicolor to grey and I never knew how free you made me until you weren't here any more. Why else do you think I got into so much trouble? I knew that I always had you to catch me.

But now I'm afraid and all I want is for everyone to be okay. That's why I cook and clean, look out for Lawrence and cover up for him. I want him to keep going without you, even though I know he's finding it almost impossible. The rest of us are muddling through. There are moments when I see the sadness in Tish's eyes, Joe's and Michael's too, but mostly we hide it from each other.

I have learned that grief is unlike any other emotion. Happiness, sadness, excitement and anger become moments that you remember only distantly when they are gone. But grief can suck you back into its chasm in a single moment. A sight, sound or smell is enough to make it wash over you as hollow as the first moment you ever felt it.

Lawrence was too young to lose you. Not a boy and not yet a man. He's floating in between and I just have to watch over him for long enough to make sure that he will be okay.

I want you to be here again. I want it so much that sometimes the pain inside me is so strong I think of putting my head through a window to stop it. But you're not and being on stage doesn't feel the same any more. How can I pretend to be someone else when each day takes everything now?

So, yes, Mum. I'm scared. And I don't want my world to change any more than it already has. If that means staying here and not going to RADA, finding a nine-to-five job that I can walk to and from, maybe bumping into Jean or Cathy on the way home or nipping in to see Dick and Bill, getting back in time for Lawrence, seeing John and keeping my world small enough to feel safe, then that is what I will do.

It was you who made me fearless.

Tish is the one who reminds me most of you. She chivvies me along, watches over me with Phil. They're always taking me out and making sure I have fun. Joe, too. He is the one who makes me laugh and looks after me. Michael guides us all, keeping us in line. But the sum of these parts does not add up to you, and all I want is to keep everything the same as it is now because then I know I will cope. I am afraid I will not be able to if anything else changes.

Lawrence walks into the kitchen and sits down as I push the letter back into my bag.

'You're up!' I say.

'Yeh.'

'About time too. You've got to go to school tomorrow, do you hear?'

'Yeh.'

He looks at me, pale and exhausted.

'I'm going to get tea on in a minute,' I say. 'But how about some Angel Delight first?'

He smiles as I walk over to the cupboard, lean down and pull out a couple of packets: strawberry for him and butterscotch for me. It is my brother's favourite pudding.

Bosch radio

There are candles stuck in Chianti bottles, red chequered tablecloths and a foot creeping up my thigh. I'm sitting at a table of about twenty work colleagues having a meal in an

Italian restaurant. Joe-from-Sales is sitting opposite me. He's got greasy black hair, a kipper tie and a smile like the Joker's. I long to tell him to fuck off. Instead I push back my chair so his stubby leg can't reach any higher up mine. With a disgruntled look on his face, he digs into his prawn cocktail.

After absentmindedly sitting my A levels and leaving St Joan's, I had got a job temping at a radio-parts warehouse on the Greycaine Industrial Estate. The work was repetitive and boring but at least I was earning more than at Boots and it was close to home.

'Take the job!' Dad had urged, when I told him that my boss Mr Bradford had offered me a permanent position soon after I'd started. 'Begin at the bottom. Just like me. You could make a good job of that, Mary.'

'But I don't want to sell radios for the rest of my life.'

'Too good for sales, are you?'

'I don't mean that. It's just boring. People ring up about all these tiny parts and I don't know what on earth they're going on about.'

'But it's time you started keeping yourself. You're eighteen. Who do you think is going to pay for you now? I'd left home by your age.'

Anger flared inside me as I looked at my father's scowling face. 'It's not as if I'm costing you much!'

'And what do you expect of me now? I was paying my own way by the time I was your age and so should you. You've got your A levels. You did okay. You can get a decent job. This is a good opportunity, Mary. Don't waste it.'

'What if I don't want it?'

'Well, you should. It's a start.'

'But I don't want the job! It's so bloody dull there.'

I stare down the table past the gaze of Joe-from-Sales and the chianti bottles. Jan-the-manageress is glaring at me from the opposite end. She's so tiny you'd step on her if you weren't looking, so pale and ginger that I swear she lights up at night. Small and feral, she has these beady eyes that are on me in a flash if the sales guys come in for a chat.

'All right, Mary!' they say, as they perch on the side of my desk to talk about what was on television last night or which pub they're going to this weekend.

'Back to work!' Jan shrieks, as she bustles up to us. 'You're far too easily distracted, Mary. Now, please concentrate for more than a minute.'

I can't be stuck on a trading estate with Jan for ever. I don't want to end up like her. She looks like she's permanently sucking a lemon.

Mr Kipling French Fancies

Her ash blonde hair has been teased so much it looks like a crash helmet and is robustly held in position by a head-band. She is wearing a cream skirt suit, pearl earrings, and her face is barely visible under a thick layer of foundation. My father's new girlfriend looks like a hybrid of Mrs Slocombe and Barbara Cartland.

'Hello, dee-aihs,' she says, in a voice clipped somewhere

between Bricket Wood and St Albans as she walks into the Front Room.

'Won't you sit down, Rebecca?' Dad asks, as he leads the way in his best suit.

The five of us have been called to attend Saturday-afternoon tea. Sitting in a line on the sofa and living-room chairs, we watch as Dad wedges his hand firmly in the small of Rebecca's back and she lowers herself slowly into the swivel chair.

'Get something nice, won't you?' he said to me yesterday, as I stared in surprise at the five-pound note he thrust into my hand. 'Cake and things. Scones maybe. And make some sandwiches, too.'

We'd heard from Phil's mum, Joyce, that Dad had been dancing with one particular woman at the Widows and Widowers Club. But I thought it would be a glamorous young widow. What does Dad see in Rebecca? She looks so old and he is still a good-looking man. But then again what does she see in a gruff Belfast man who drives a Rover when she'd expect a Jaguar at least by the look of her?

'I'll make a pot of tea, then, shall I, sweetheart?' Dad says, and bolts out of the room.

The clock ticks. The canary starts to sing.

'Would you like a cake while you're waiting?' Tish says eventually.

'Why, thank you, dee-aih.'

Rebecca bites delicately into a yellow French Fancy. Wearing blue eye shadow and red lipstick, she looks like a giant mouse in drag nibbling cheese. I think of the delicate stroke of coral lipstick that Mum used to wear.

'Very nice,' Rebecca says, as she looks at Tish. 'Although I do love Marks & Spencer's cakes.'

My father reappears with the teapot and starts to fill cups. 'How about another wee cake, darling?'

'Thank you, Sam.'

Rebecca sits bolt upright. Her feet – clad in cream patent shoes – are neatly placed one beside the other. I wonder if she smells of violets.

'Are you going to show Rebecca the pigeon loft, Dad?' Joe asks.

My father's face reddens. 'She doesn't want to be seeing that now, Joe.'

How long are we going to have to sit here? John is taking me out later and I want to wash my hair. Since meeting him, I seem to spend half my life washing my hair and the other shaving my legs.

'Well, isn't this grand?' Dad says. 'How about another cup of tea?'

Rebecca dabs the corners of her mouth as he pours.

'I'm glad you're here with us, darling,' Dad says.

'And so am I, Sam. It's been a hard year for you but you've done such a wonderful job. Look how well you've done. Five children to bring up all on your own. They must run you ragged.'

We stare at each other as she takes a sip of tea.

'I have to confess that I couldn't look after so many. My Raymond is such a good boy. No trouble at all. I'm always saying how lucky I am. There's no mistake. A mother couldn't ask for more.'

'And a lovely boy he is,' Dad says. 'No doubt about it. He's about your age, Lawrence. You should meet him.'

My brother stares mutely at Dad. Rebecca raises a hand to pat her hair, as if to check that the carapace of Elnett hasn't failed.

'Do you want me to get you an ashtray?' Tish asks Dad.

He delves into his pocket, takes out a packet of Polos and hurls one into his mouth.

'And what would I be wanting that for, seeing as how I don't smoke?' he hisses. We look at each other in confusion. Rebecca stares at Dad. Her mouth twists into a grimace of a smile.

I wonder how long it will take for her to go the way of Bernadette.

Moving on

On a cool September morning I walk into Cassio College where the faint tang of bleach hangs in the air.

I phoned the college last week in a haphazard attempt to get out of working at Bosch for the rest of my life. After making friends with Alan, the guy who designed signage and advertising materials for the salesmen, I'd often chatted to him in his studio. It was full of ink, pens, paint and glue, and I'd decided that graphics seemed an okay job because at least you got to draw and be a bit creative. After drama, my second love was art.

'You need to get onto a course,' Alan had told me. 'There's one at the art school in Harrow. Or you could try Cassio College in Watford.'

Days before the start of term, I'd phoned Cassio and a woman had told me someone had dropped off the course at the last minute. 'This doesn't usually happen,' she said. 'It's an HND course. One of the best there is. Our students go all over. Can you come for an interview tomorrow?'

'Of course.'

'One thing, though: we only do graphics with visual merchandising.'

'What's that?'

'Shop windows. You'll learn everything there is to know about how to put windows together. Like those big ones you see in Clements, dear. Props and lighting, signage, things like that.'

I didn't have a clue what she was talking about and I certainly didn't want to work in a shop for the rest of my life. But Cassio was local. It was the only kind of way out that I could hope for right now.

'Y.M.C.A.' by the Village People

'Never underestimate the power of polystyrene,' said Mr Lawrence. 'You should have seen what I used to do with it in the Christmas grotto.'

Brown suit, Craven A fag and decades of experience at

Cordells department store, Mr Lawrence was in charge of teaching us about creating signage and props. We put them into mocked-up shop windows every Friday, and the rest of the week was spent working towards that moment. In a studio filled with ten-foot-high black boxes that doubled as windows, we painted and sprayed backdrops before installing the props we'd made and placing the product that formed the centrepiece of our windows. One week we'd do a soup display, the next china and towels; kitchenware was followed by Grand Marnier.

Sally, who wore Kicker boots and had worked in beauty, was responsible for overseeing the creation of our windows. Alan Springhall was the man who helped design them first on paper by teaching us to make 3D drawings of our displays. I had quickly realized that graphics required an attention to the most minute detail that I would never possess. A lot of girls fancied Mr Springhall – he was at least a decade younger than most of the lecturers and had a camera permanently slung round his neck – but, then again, they would because they were mostly sixteen. Two years can feel like a lifetime when you are eighteen and even more so when you still cry as your old school bus goes past because you so desperately miss the one constant you had after your mother's death.

Cassio didn't stand a chance. I put a hard shell around me as I tried to adapt to change and adopted a dismissive air to everyone and everything. My fellow students were young and small-town, I decided. I was running a home while they were talking about pocket money; I was going up to Kensington

Market at the weekends while they were still shopping at Chelsea Girl; I was worrying about getting my younger brother out of bed in the mornings, they were arguing with theirs; I was going to clubs like the Roxy in Soho where Siouxsie Sioux & the Banshees, the Clash and the Jam played while my classmates were still at the New Penny.

'So what are you going to put in your window tomorrow?' a girl called Tracy had asked me, as we queued in the canteen for a coffee.

'Blondie. *Parallel Lines.*'

She had crashed onto the scene in a blaze of peroxide, red lips and ripped T-shirts, and I was besotted with her: the insouciance, the disdain, the girl with a one-of-the-boys attitude. Joe had bleached and blunt-chopped my hair and I'd started tie-dyeing jeans on the sly in the photography dark room at Cassio during my lunch breaks. Our windows tomorrow had to be about music and I was planning to paint mine with black and white lines, like a zebra crossing. A mannequin sprayed white with a single black line covering its eyes would stand in the corner next to albums suspended in a zigzag across the window.

'How about you?' I asked Tracy.

'The Village People.'

I stared at her. 'But the brief is about music and innovation. You think "Y.M.C.A." is innovative?'

'Yeh.'

I sighed as I looked at my new friend Danielle. The same age as me, her idol was Lauren Bacall and she wore vintage fur coats, permanently had a packet of B&H in her hand and often turned up for college wearing last night's eyeliner. Her French mother, Suzette, was an antiques dealer, who made things like chicken livers in red wine sauce. Her dad was a cameraman and so good-looking he'd been in an Opal Fruits commercial. Her sister Michelle danced brilliantly to 'Hit Me With Your Rhythm Stick'. These were interesting people doing interesting things. Danielle and I had gone to see *Midnight Express* yesterday at the cinema. Tracy would have been first in line for a ticket to *Watership Down*.

'The Village People aren't innovative!' I snorted. 'You think a few blokes dancing around in fancy dress is new?'

'Well, no one's done it before.'

'Because it's shit. It's not innovative. It's just bad taste.'

Tracy's hand quivered as the dinner lady handed her a cup of Maxwell House. 'Just because it's not your taste doesn't mean it's bad.'

'And that's yours? Seriously? The Village People? It's not going to inspire anyone.'

'And how do you know that?'

'Because "Y.M.C.A." is naff.'

'So what do you think is good taste then, if you're such an expert?'

'Loads of people. Siouxsie & the Banshees. Donna Summer. Elvis Costello. Bowie.'

'But Bowie did a comedy song! What about "Laughing Gnome"?'

'It was a one-off!' I roared. 'He was being kooky.'

'So if Bowie does it, it's okay?' Tracy yelled. 'You're just a snob.'

'I'm not a bloody snob. I just know what's good music and what's not.'

'You think you know it all but you don't. That's your trouble, Mary.'

And it was. Grief had found the perfect outlet in disdain for everyone and everything around me at Cassio.

Fiat 500

John and I walk into the station car park and head towards his car. We haven't spoken much on the way back from the theatre in London.

We get into his battered car. Sitting down, I feel the familiar lurch of the passenger seat falling out of position. As usual, I'm half sitting, half lying down. I've spent months driving around peeping over the dashboard of his Fiat 500.

'So what did you think?' John says, as he looks down at me.

'It was all right.'

'All right?'

'Yeh. All right.'

He probably loved it, I think. John is so clever and well read. He works as a union negotiator and keeps telling me that a woman called Margaret Thatcher might be elected next year. This is apparently bad news but I've got no clue what he's on about. There are so many things I don't understand that John does. Politics. The fact that you can eat the rind of Brie instead of cutting it off. *Waiting for Godot.*

But I can't tell him that, can I? We've just spent three hours watching it. Thank God the drama group we've joined doesn't do Beckett plays. John persuaded me to start acting again and we've joined the Bushey and Oxhey Amateur Dramatics Society. I'm glad he did because I've missed acting ever since turning down RADA. Danielle is a member, too, and we've made friends with Guy and Liz, Roger and Tor. Gay and Andy have even invited us for 'supper' around their kitchen table.

We're doing *Dick Whittington* for the Christmas panto in a few weeks. It's simple: a pussy, a principal boy and a dame.

John takes my hand. 'I thought that play was a pile of shit,' he says.

Warmth fills me.

Creosote

My father has started to wash his own underpants, putting them into a pot and bringing them to the boil on the cooker with a handful of Daz.

There are other changes, too. He's bought a pair of slip-on shoes and is out so much that we can go days without seeing him properly. On weekends, he visits Rebecca and often insists that Lawrence goes with him.

'You can keep Raymond company while we go out for a bite to eat,' he tells Lawrence, most Friday mornings.

'Raymond needs a babysitter, does he?' Joe asks.

'Rebecca doesn't want him alone in the house.'

'But what about Lawrence? He hates going over there.'

'No, he doesn't.'

'Yes, he does, Dad. He says Raymond is a mummy's boy and he's got nothing in common with him. So why do you keep making him go? And why did you give his skateboard to Raymond for that matter?'

'Ach. He's too old for that now, Joe.'

'He's not. It's his favourite thing.'

'Lawrence is nearly sixteen. Far too old for skateboards.'

'But why do you keep giving his stuff to Raymond? He doesn't have much and now you're giving it away.'

'Enough, Joe! If I want to give Rebecca or Raymond or anyone else something from this house, then it is mine to give. Do you hear?'

After months of ignoring his birds, I had found Dad creosoting the pigeon loft last weekend. Wearing his old garden jacket with a paintbrush in his hand and a Player's hanging out of the corner of his mouth, he looked suddenly familiar again.

'All right, Dad?' I said, as I walked outside.

'I'm getting the loft ready. I'm selling up.'

'What do you mean?'

'It's all going to go. I've had enough. I'm getting it ready and then I'll put an ad in the *Watford Observer*.'

'But why? You love your birds, Dad.'

'Not any more. I've had my fun with them but now it's over.'

I thought of Rebecca: the cream suit and perfect hair; the

shoes that matched the outfit and the plastic runners that probably covered her carpets at home.

Then I thought of my mother.

'Close the door,' she would call, if one of us left it open on a cold day. 'It's icy, that wind. Stepmother's breath, that is. You'll catch your death.'

Brillo pads

I have filled my Friday windows with tins of Campbell's soup, bottles of Brut and cases of Liebfraumilch, hung six-foot lengths of fuchsia, red and orange paper from the ceiling and torn rips in it through which peep china products. I have woven strands of wool like a giant cat's cradle and suspended bottles of perfume in them like baubles on a Christmas tree. I have dreamed up ideas for kitchenware and sports clothing, bathroom accessories and lighting, baking products, soap and back-to-school stationery.

The rest of the week passes me by. Walking into college in the morning, I wait for the moment when I can leave again. I sit in lectures on retail commerce and art history, thinking about what jobs I need to do at home or seeing John. I worry about Lawrence as teachers talk. I have no interest in learning skills like prop-making and handwriting signage. I'm never going to work in a shop. I'm just biding my time.

Some days I don't even turn up for college at all. Usually I go over to Danielle's house and we smoke cigarettes as we go through the bottles in her parents' drinks cabinet: sherry and dry martini, Advocaat and whisky, vodka, gin and Bacardi. I live for life outside college when I am with John, my brothers, Tish and Phil, Danielle, and a new friend we've made at Cassio called Suzanne. These are the moments when the anger whirling inside me is stilled.

We go up to London to look at buckled boots in Shelly's, hunt in second-hand shops for old men's work jackets to wear with ripped jeans, or drive out to country pubs for a drink. We visit clubs like Global Village on Embankment or eat the Sunday roasts that I cook with Tish while everyone piles into the living room just like they did when Mum was alive. Punk has segued into New Wave and Vivienne Westwood is selling bondage trousers at Seditionaries on the King's Road. Compared to this colourful world of music, fashion and colour, Cassio feels like it will kill me with grey.

Dora Reeve, the woman in charge of the course, knows it. She is proud of the work she does at Cassio and the students she turns out. She likes the girls from Abbots Langley and St Albans, who diligently make notes in class and write essays. Having worked in luxury before starting to teach at Cassio, she still carries it with her in a spritz of L'Air du Temps and the Cacharel cardigans she wears. Dora knows that retail is a world of hard work and attention to detail. You will never succeed if you don't fully apply yourself.

'Have you cleaned up the studio?' she asks me, one Friday afternoon.

I have spent hours spray-painting old pairs of shoes that I got from second-hand shops all over Watford. Stacking

All of Mum's friends came in and had their hair done for free by Joe. It was a chance to see them, have a cup of tea and catch up on news.

'All Harry does these days is watch golf,' Sheila would tell me. 'It only takes him a few hours to read the gas meters and then he's home under my feet. I preferred it when he was on the buses.'

Local girls, like Jackie, Joanne, Annette, Carolyn and Loretta, became our friends. They were always popping in to get their hair done and tell us what pub or club they were going to that night. Seriously interested in fashion and haircuts, they had jobs whose sole purpose was to earn them enough to pay for the weekends. Mark, the colourist, also spent all his money on fashion. He was obsessed with Vivienne Westwood and permanently in a pair of bondage trousers. Lynn, the stylist, had a blonde pixie, wore baggy jodhpurs and slouched behind her clients as if she was waiting for a bus. Terry looked like a young Clint Eastwood.

Everyone had a fashion tribe and it seemed there were no rules. Soul boys in Hawaiian shirts and jelly shoes; Rockabilly boys wearing vintage Levi's with checked lumberjack shirts; girls in peg trousers and baggy white shirts; both sexes in denim dungarees with a woollen hat wedged on the back of their head and a leather workman's jacket. Time and effort went into creating looks, and those without money scoured Camden and other markets while those with a wage headed to the King's Road or Kensington.

But there was one shop unlike any other, and even though it didn't contain a stitch of clothing, Joe and I had walked open-mouthed through Habitat when it opened in Watford. Did people really have houses that looked like something from Scandinavia and were filled with pasta jars? When he bought me a white bedspread, I swore I'd never actually sleep under it.

Unexpected news

Michael, Tish, Joe, Lawrence and I sit wordlessly in the living room listening to raised voices in the kitchen.

'What are you thinking, Sam?' Aunty Cathy says. 'You can't just up and leave them. Where will they go? What will they do?'

'They're adults, Cath. It's time to make their own way.'

'But Mary is still studying. Lawrence hasn't even left school.'

'He will soon enough. He's joining the police cadets and then, when he's old enough, he'll become an officer. It's a good career and Dunstable is too far away to commute into school around here so he can't move in with me. He's going to apply and start in a few months.'

'But he's only sixteen, Sam! He's still grieving for his mother. And if Lawrence thinks that you don't want him then of course he's going to agree to sign up. What are you thinking of?'

'Rebecca and I want to make a life together. The kids don't need us now.'

'Of course they do.'

'They're adults, Cath. They'll all be gone soon, and what will I do in this house alone? Tish and Michael have already moved on. Joe's more than old enough to get his own place. Mary's eighteen. An adult. And Lawrence wants to go.'

'But this is ridiculous! What would Theresa say if she was here?'

'Without being bloody rude, I think you should keep your nose out of it, Cathy. I've got a chance. I need the money from this house if Rebecca and I are going to move. I've worked hard enough for it.'

'Be that as it may, what you're doing is wrong. And I for one am not going to sit by and say nothing.'

'Well, I'd thank you to keep your opinions to YOURSELF,' roars Dad.

The door to the kitchen is wrenched open and we hear Aunty Cathy's steps in the hallway. The front door slams and then there is silence.

Dad has finally taken leave of his senses. We should have seen it coming but we were sure he would realize how mismatched they were and that Rebecca would disappear as quickly from Dad's life as rapidly as she had appeared in it. But this shadowy figure, a person we never see or speak to, a woman we hardly know, is seemingly in charge now.

We all know Dad thinks he's in love but he's clutching at straws. Rebecca is something to hold onto without Mum. But doesn't he understand that she will never replace her? Where Mum was soft, Rebecca is hard; where Mum was warm, she is cold; where Mum laughed, she is humourless. There is no one who could be less like the woman Dad cherished for so many years. I understand that he never really had a family before Mum came along. Dad's mother died when he was young and he was brought up by a housekeeper. He never really knew what family was until Mum gave him one and then he lost her.

I want to be patient. But all I feel is rage that Lawrence is being pushed into joining the police cadets when anyone can see it's the last thing he should be doing.

'Can't you see how he's struggling?' I'd demanded, when Dad spoke to us a few days ago.

'Aren't we all?'

'You're a joke,' I said hotly. 'You can't sell this house and leave us nowhere to go.'

'You're being hysterical, Mary. You're old enough to look after yourself.'

'But I'm still at college. What will I do for money?'

'You had that job offer at Bosch and turned it down. You'll find somewhere and you can start earning. I've got a new life now with Rebecca and I can't have two women in my kitchen.'

'I didn't plan on being in it for ever,' I screamed. 'Let her bloody take over. In her posh clothes and high heels.'

As Joe rounded on Dad, rage written across his features, the atmosphere in the room snapped. 'You're a fucking embarrassment,' he snarled.

'Joe!' Michael yelled. 'Listen to me, Dad. Selling the house isn't the answer. This is ridiculous.'

'DON'T YOU DARE TALK TO ME LIKE THIS!' Dad bellowed. 'I WILL NOT HAVE IT.'

'Why not, Dad?' Tish said.

We looked at her in surprise. Tish and my father never argued.

'This is our last link with Mum,' she said, as she started to sob. 'Where will we go?'

'You're not even living here any more! You and Phil are engaged. You'll be getting your own place soon. I'm supposed to keep this house on just so you can visit, am I?'

'But what about Mary and Lawrence? All you ever think of is yourself.'

'Don't you dare backchat me!' Dad screamed. 'That's enough!'

We haven't spoken about it since. Silence has settled over the house but the air is tense, meals are hurriedly eaten without a word before everyone goes their separate ways. Joe and I huddle in my bedroom to chat about it.

'What is he thinking of?' I say.

'No idea. I don't know what he sees in her. Doesn't he realize how ridiculous he is? He's an embarrassment.'

'But what are we going to do? Where are we going to go?'

'Dunno. Let's hope it takes ages to sell this place. We'll work something out.'

'You're sure, Joe?'

'Course I am,' he replies, as he gives me a hug. 'I can afford somewhere. We can stick together.'

But no one can make Dad see sense. Not even Don and Harry.

'This is her doing,' they mutter, when they come over.

But it isn't. Not really. Dad is our father. And I don't feel angry or sad about what he's doing. I just feel ashamed. I don't want anyone to know what is happening. Surely they will think that we must have done something to deserve this. Because, if not, what kind of father makes his own children homeless?

Hotpoint fridge

Michael, Joe, Tish, Lawrence and I draw closer and closer together. We're such a tight-knit group that the only out-siders we let in are John and Phil. We eat and laugh together, socialize, argue and look out for one another. We move as a tribe because we're all each other has got.

Joe and I took Lawrence to my friend Jackie's house party not long ago and a bloke started chatting me up in the kitchen.

'Stuck-up bitch,' he'd slurred, when he realized he wasn't getting anywhere. 'Think you're so high and mighty, do you? Fucking skinny cow.'

The next thing I knew, Lawrence had lifted the guy off his feet. As he pinned him to the fridge, Joe threw a single punch. The man slumped in a heap as my brothers looked at me with fire in their eyes.

Harvey Nichols

It is the smell that hits me first as I walk through the store doors: a blend of sweet leather and perfume, plus the sharp tang of starch. As I look at ladies with blue rinses and delicate marcasite brooches pinned to cashmere cardigans browsing display cabinets, I know what I am smelling: money.

Dora had seemed reluctant when I'd asked her if I could go to Harrods during my work-experience placement at the end of my first year at Cassio.

'I know you want to go there with Danielle,' she said. 'But she at least has put some effort into this course, which is why I've put her forward. You have not.'

'Well, I can't go to Clements. My dad works there.'

'How about Miss Selfridge?'

'No! I don't want to work on the high street. I want to go to a big department store.'

At least then I could go to see Tish at UCH when I finished work or nip to World's End to look at the shops with Danielle.

'Very well, then,' Dora said, with a sigh. 'If you really insist, then I know someone at Harvey Nichols. But please make sure you apply yourself, Mary. We have a reputation at Cassio and I don't want you to damage it.'

I stand looking around as a doorman stares at me. I am wearing red Kicker boots, dungarees and my hair has been sprayed so much that a gale-force wind won't make an impact.

'Can I help you, madam?' he says.

'I'm here on work experience with the display team.'

'Then you need to use the staff entrance in Harriet Walk. Go down the stairs into the basement and straight ahead. The studio is at the end of the corridor. You'll find them all in there.'

Five minutes later, I walk into a huge room filled with noise and activity. A radio is playing and the air smells of glue and paint. Men in brown coats are pushing trolleys filled with rolls of fabric as people run around with hammers, staple guns and tool kits. In the middle of the room, a tall guy with bright red hair is wearing a feather headdress and the tightest drainpipes I've ever seen. With a glue gun in his hand, he dances like Salome with her veil in front of a mannequin whose face is covered with beads.

'We've got to get her into some Janice Wainwright and up to the Evening and After Sex department,' he drawls.

Spinning around, he spots me. 'Oh, hello. Are you the work-experience girl, then?'

The only other man I've ever heard speak like him is Larry Grayson.

'Yup,' I say.

'Oh, good!' he replies, with a smile. 'Now, what rotten job can we give you?'

'Not so fast,' another voice calls, and I turn to see a man of about thirty walking towards me.

With sandy-coloured hair and a warm gentle smile, his woollen suit is cut like a glove and he is wearing beautiful tasselled oxblood loafers. He is the most glamorous thing I've ever seen. 'So you're the girl from Cassio?'

'Yeh. I'm Mary. Mary Newton.'

'Good to meet you. I'm Andrew. Now why don't you come into my office?'

He leads me to a small room unlike any office I've ever seen. The walls are draped in fabric, there are candles and lamps everywhere, and bookshelves stacked with names like Fortuny, Helmut Newton and Cecil Beaton. Andrew gestures me into a chair.

'You're here for two weeks, aren't you?'

'Yes.'

'First work experience?'

'Yes.'

'Nervous?'

'Yes.'

'I felt exactly the same when I was at Cassio.'

'You're from Watford?'

'Oh, yes, darling,' he says, flicking back his sandy hair. 'I hide it well, though, don't I? I'm in charge of all this. I'm the display manager.'

He smiles kindly as he leans back in his chair, rolling a black Mont Blanc fountain pen between his fingers.

'Now, soon enough we'll find you something to do,' Andrew says. 'But first things first: how on earth are you surviving at that God-awful college?'

I fall straight in love.

Hermès scarf

Harvey Nichols was like a Rolls Royce: classic, comfortable and reassuringly expensive. The store of choice for the *grandes dames* of Knightsbridge, all they asked in return for their unwavering loyalty was understated and dependable luxury. They didn't want high fashion. They expected discreet expense, the kind that didn't scream money but whispered it, using cashmere, pearls and kid leather.

The twenty-strong display team was responsible for showcasing everything that Harvey Nichols had in store. They were made up of a mixture of understatedly chic men – like Andrew and his assistant, Paul, who talked in a voice honed by private school and sat in an office lined with books about architecture – young people dressed in the latest fashions, and screaming queens, whose barbs and histrionic mood swings were delivered with razor-sharp wit. These men were as exotic to me as Marc Bolan had once been. Homosexuality had only been decriminalized twelve years before and it had not yet reached Watford, as far as I knew.

One tier below Andrew and Paul were the senior dressers and under them a team of juniors, who toiled like worker bees serving their queens. Huge store-front windows had to be filled to entice passers-by inside; mannequins styled and placed at the top of escalators to beckon people into departments; pedestals topped with products that customers had never known they wanted until they saw them; glass cabinets stuffed like treasure boxes to make people stop and stare.

The studio was the hub of the process, the place where everything that would bring the designs to life was stored or made. Mannequins were stacked – some naked, others wearing wigs but all ready to be transformed into a fantasy – beside huge bales of felt in every colour waiting to be stapled onto window floors, walls and ceilings to create backdrops. There were rolls of PVC and wire netting; shelves of shoes, socks, hosiery; boxes of props ranging from Japanese paper umbrellas, Spanish fans and Venetian carnival masks to lights, feathers and gilt cherubs.

The process started with the senior dressers making a three-dimensional drawing of the window that was signed off by Andrew and Paul. Then everything that was needed to fill it was prepared – props were made and products signed out from every department by the juniors.

'I've got the Dunhill jumper from Menswear,' they'd call to whomever they were assisting.

'What colour?'

'Pale yellow.'

'But I need sunshine! Think of the Côte d'Azur. Not your Aunt Ethel's lemon curd. Now go and find me something else.'

The radio was constantly on, ironing boards up and steamers going. Senior dressers pinning, pleating and styling while their juniors clutched tool kits containing display wire, a glue gun, hammer, nails and double-sided tape, ready to fix a product into place at the arching of an eyebrow. When everything was ready the dressing teams would head off into the store to install the displays.

As people worked, I heard them chatting about what clubs and bars they'd been to, what theatre and exhibitions they'd seen and which clothes they were saving up to buy. It was a world of fashion, music and experimentation.

'I swear I'm going to have that Loewe belt if it kills me,' a dresser would sigh. 'I've not eaten for days. But I've lost an inch off my waist and saved myself three quid.'

As I stared at the huge store-front windows at the end of the day, I suddenly glimpsed the possibility that Cassio might offer for the first time. Sitting in a lecture, I'd heard that Salvador Dalí had designed windows. So had Andy Warhol. Now I understood why. These windows were art, drama, a fantasy landscape where anything could be played out, a performance. They were a stage, and through them the audience of passers-by were transported just as they were when they watched a play. My love of drama had found a new outlet.

Suddenly the final year at Cassio didn't seem like a prison sentence any more as I worked in the studio making cups of tea, sweeping the floors and occasionally getting out a glue gun to stick something together. If I could work somewhere like this – a place where dreams were played out in the windows, rather than sticking a T-shirt on a mannequin at Chelsea Girl – I wanted to do it. But while I was desperate for a chance to put some of the ideas I had into practice, I didn't get a chance to go near a display until my final day.

'I've got you an accessory case by door number five,' Duncan the redhead says, as he walks up to me.

'What do you mean?'

'I mean you've been chirping like a budgie ever since you got here so let's see what you can do on your own, shall we?'

'But what do you want in it?'

'Anything you like.'

We walk up the staff stairs and onto the ground floor where we stop in front of a two-foot-wide glass display case close to one of the back doors.

'Everyone who parks in Harriet Walk or Cadogan Place walks in here and past this case so don't mess it up,' Duncan says. 'Any problems, I'll be up on the first floor. I'll come and find you in an hour.'

'But what do I do?'

'It's simple, darling. Make it sing!'

With a wink, he turns on his heel and leaves me staring at the accessory department.

There are scarves and belts, wallets and jewellery, small leather goods, fountain pens and fragrances. Walking around the floor, I peer into glass-topped counters as I wonder what to put in my case. A pile of colourful silk scarves catches my eye. They remind me of the silk ties that I loved as a kid when I visited Austin Reed with Dad. One in particular stands out: orange, yellow and red. I pick it up and feel it slip between my fingers. The softest silk. The label says 'Hermès'.

'Can I sign this one out, please?' I say to a sales assistant standing behind the counter. 'I'm doing the display case by door five.'

She purses her lips as she looks at me. 'We're trying to push the Chopard,' she replies. 'Can't you use one of those?'

For a moment, I almost falter. But already a picture is forming in my mind. 'Sorry, but I need that one.'

With a sigh, she hands it to me and I fill out a chit for her to sign. A clutch bag in conker brown crocodile and a red Yves Saint Laurent lipstick are soon added to my pile. After walking down to the studio and attaching the chits to the notice-board listing what product has been signed out by whom, I get myself a tool belt and cut some pieces of yellow felt. With shaking legs, I walk back upstairs, open the case, and line the bottom with the felt, gluing it in place.

Then I take the display wire out of my tool belt.

Wiring fabric is one of the most important skills that a visual merchandiser can have. It sounds simple enough: just thread a hair thin wire along a seam and then mould it into whatever shape you want the fabric to follow. But while anyone can stick wire into a hem and make do, only the really talented can wire a product so delicately, so precisely, that the colour, pile and cut suddenly become three-dimensional as the fabric takes on a life of its own.

Unrolling the wire, I carefully start to thread it into the seam of the scarf. If I mess this up, I will never be able to set foot in this shop again. With shaking hands, I place the crocodile clutch half open at the back of the case and gently put the unwired side of the scarf into it. Then I arrange the wired section so that it cascades out of the clutch like snakes slithering across the bottom of the case. The lipstick stands livid red in the front right corner. A calfskin wallet is laid beside it. I stand back and wait for Duncan. I want him to think of a sunrise, see the scarf streaming out of the bag as the first rays.

Duncan stops six feet from the box and narrows his gaze. Then he walks up to the case, bends down and stares again. 'It's good,' he says, with a smile. 'The scarf needs a bit of work but you've got some talent, haven't you, darling?'

'You like it?'

'Yes. I do. Now let's nip out and see what Harrods has done today with those shithole windows of hers, shall we?'

Clearasil cleanser

Everything was changing as the 1970s drew to a close: the Winter of Discontent saw Margaret Thatcher swept to power and Sid Vicious overdose in a blaze of publicity. Earl Mountbatten was blown up off the coast of Ireland, and a killer dubbed the Yorkshire Ripper terrorized women.

But time was suspended in Windsor Road as we waited to see what would happen with the house and where we would go. Dad stayed more and more at Rebecca's after the estate agent's board went up. Coming home only to drop off some money for food and give me a bag of his washing, he'd look nervously around before leaving again. Once he appeared with a cuddly Womble he'd bought at Clements.

'Thought you might like it,' he said, as he handed it to me and I stared at the cuddly toy, wondering why my father would think it was appropriate for a daughter he kept insisting was old enough to fend completely for herself.

The air between us hummed, yet neither of us said a word. I dreaded the moment when I heard the familiar thrum of his Rover outside. I dreaded the moment when I heard it disappear into the distance again.

Despite what had happened at Harvey Nichols, there were many days when I stayed in bed instead of going into college. Lying underneath the blankets, I'd hear the phone ring and reluctantly go downstairs to pick it up.

'Can I speak to Mr Newton, please? It's Matthew from Rennies Estate Agents.'

'He's not here. Can I help?'

'I've got a couple who want to see the house. Can I bring them over tonight, please?'

Some days the phone rang several times and each time it did I'd reluctantly agree to show people around. Couples would appear on the doorstep, smiling eagerly before walking around and peering into cupboards as they discussed what colour they'd paint the walls. As I listened to them, I did not trust myself to speak. I knew the house would sell soon and I had hoped that I could move in with Tish and Phil. But while I often went to stay in the two-bed maisonette they'd bought around the corner in Leavesden Road, I knew I couldn't stay there permanently. It was tiny and they were starting a new life together. My sister would have done anything for me but I couldn't ask her that.

I dreaded the thought of Lawrence leaving for the police cadets. He was going to the Metropolitan Police Academy in Hendon initially and would then move to Sunbury-on-Thames to do more training. After turning eighteen, he'd train to be an officer proper and I wished I could protect him from a path that I feared wasn't right for him. Music was Lawrence's passion. He listened to John Peel religiously, bought all the latest releases and took me off to see gigs by new bands like the Cure. Standing watching Robert Smith, with his wonky red lipstick and nest of hair, Lawrence was truly happy. Then he looked at me and laughed.

'You look like a budgie, Mary,' he said, as he stared at the cropped haircut that Joe had recently dyed green, blue and yellow.

Lawrence wanted to be a sound engineer or a producer. Instead Dad had convinced him that becoming a police officer was the right thing. A. Good. Steady. Job.

By the time Lawrence left for Hendon, Dad had proposed to Rebecca. The thought of being without my brother made me feel hollow as I packed up his wash bag with a bottle of Clearasil and some toothpaste. Looking after him had given me structure ever since Mum's death and now he was leaving. I'd baked him a coffee cake, made sure he'd had a haircut and hugged him for what felt like the final time.

We all took him to Hendon, cramming into his room as he looked around and tried to smile. Holding him tightly, I said goodbye.

'Don't worry about me, Mary,' Lawrence said. 'I'll be fine. I'm not a baby, you know.'

John was waiting at the house when we got home. He'd brought me a box of chocolates and followed me as I walked into the kitchen where I took out the mop and bucket.

'Joe and I are going to clean,' I said. 'I want the house to be clean.'

'Shall I give you a hand?'

'Okay, then.'

He walked up to me and pulled me into his arms. 'You okay?' he said. 'There's a good film on TV tonight. Jack Lemmon. It should be funny. Why don't we watch that?'

I breathed in his familiar scent and told myself that everything was going to be fine.

Two months later Andrew called from Harvey Nichols and offered me two weeks' paid work in December. As the store doors closed on Christmas Eve, he said that he would give me a job when I left Cassio.

Cookery In Colour by Marguerite Patten

My father's wedding is quiet, very civilized. Rebecca is a Seventh Day Adventist and suddenly Dad is one too. Even so, he is wearing the best suit in church. Silver-grey mohair. He's always known how to dress.

Michael has tried to talk to Dad in the run-up to today. Walking out of my bedroom, I have heard their voices downstairs.

'You don't need to do this, Dad,' Michael said, in a low voice. 'Sell the house if you want, but marriage? It's too soon. You're rushing into this.'

'I'm not, son. You kids have got your lives ahead of you. Rebecca is a good woman.'

'I'm not saying she isn't, Dad. But we hardly know her. And neither do you. It's too quick. It's only been a couple of years since you lost Mum.'

'I know. But she's gone and this is my chance.'

'I understand, Dad. I really do. You don't want to be left alone without us. Without Mum. But you're not thinking properly. Please reconsider.'

'Why can't you kids just accept that I'm happy?'

'Because you're not, Dad. You think you are but you're not.'

'And how would you know that?'

'I know you, Dad. We can all see. Just slow down. Please. I'm begging you.'

'No, Michael. I'm going to marry Rebecca. I've made my decision. And you kids can either accept it or not. It's your choice.'

The reception – just a quiet lunch – is held at the Noke Hotel in St Albans. Don, Sadie, Sheila, Harry and the five of us silently chew our way through prawn cocktail, silverside beef and Pavlova before walking outside to wave off the newly-weds. When the gear stick on Dad's car breaks and he has to phone a taxi, Rebecca's face sets in a rictus grin as they wait for it to take them away to their new life.

We are all adjusting to new beginnings. The house has finally been sold and I've packed up a couple of boxes but can't take too much because I am not sure where I will end up. I am staying for now with Sheila and Harry but don't know how long I'll be there and can't go humping a string of suitcases around the place. Joe has moved in with Don and Sadie but at weekends when Lawrence and Michael are home the four of us will cram into Tish's flat. Our mother's pride is dug deep inside us: we all feel embarrassed at having to ask people to put roofs over our heads. At least we can leave them in peace on the weekends when we are all together at Tish's.

And so I've packed a suitcase with some essentials, like clothes and toiletries, before filling a box with records and books that Tish is going to store. Her flat is tiny so all she can have is one box from each of us. The only things of Mum's that I have taken are her statue of St Therese of the Roses and the Marguerite Patten cookery book. Otherwise Dad has all her things at the new home in Dunstable that he is now sharing with Rebecca. The last traces of our life together have gone.

As I watch them drive away, I wonder what Dad's life will be like now that we are no longer in it. It is clear that we will hardly see him. But something shifts inside me as I watch the taxi putter down the drive. There will be no more hoping that Dad might come through, no more arguing with him about money, the house or his responsibilities to us. He has made his choice and we are on our own. I feel free.

Youth Dew

As a child I had no idea what my mother was talking about when she came out with a string of idioms.

'Dick Froome was pulling my leg today when I went into the shop,' she'd tell Dad, with a laugh.

Staring at her in surprise, I'd imagine Mr Froome tugging at Mum as she chose which Cheddar to buy.

'Least said soonest mended,' she'd advise, when I was arguing with Joe and would only stop long enough to let her speak before screaming again.

'I wish he'd put a cork in it,' she'd say, when Bob Monkhouse came on the TV. I'd shudder at the thought of where the cork would go.

But there was only one saying that I should have learned the meaning of: pride comes before a fall. My job offer at Harvey Nichols increased my disinterest in my college course, and the only thing I put any effort into was creating the Friday windows – and my endless battle of wills with Dora Reeve.

'How could you?' she'd screeched, one day, as we stood in the studio. 'Do you know how much these mannequins cost?'

I stared at her, feeling laughter about to explode. 'It was just a joke!'

'But it isn't funny. This is an Adel Rootstein mannequin. Do you realize what that means? And look what you've done to it!'

It was a Friday afternoon and Dora was due to mark what we'd produced that week. But during our lunch break, I'd nipped back to the studio and plonked a naked mannequin into Danielle's window. Then I'd cut a piece off a red wig and stuck it on the mannequin's crotch.

Dora Reeve had bright red hair.

Adel Rootstein mannequins are worth thousands. They are works of art in themselves, so lifelike and graceful that she supplies all the world's top stores. Cassio was lucky enough to be given old mannequins when shops bought Adel's new collection because she was constantly updating the look of her product, just as fashion houses did. Adel created manne-quins to resemble the hottest models so when some fell out

of fashion they were passed on to places like Cassio. Dora
cherished those mannequins like children.

'How you think you will ever make a career when you
behave like this is beyond me,' she said. 'Now clear this up
and there will be serious consequences if you ever damage
college property like this again.'

But I felt protected by knowing that I had a job to go to. I
wasn't going to listen to Dora but I should have known better.
Soon I was knocking on her door after Andrew phoned to tell
me that he could no longer give me the job. Harvey Nichols
had implemented a recruitment freeze and now I had nothing
to go to when I left Cassio.

'I'm so sorry, Mary,' he said. 'There's nothing I can do.
They're not letting us hire anyone. But if anything changes I'll
let you know. We'd love to have you here with us.'

There was only one solution: Harrods. Danielle had got a
job there after doing her work experience and I had to convince them to give me one too, if I could get an interview.
Maybe all the trainee places would be filled by now. But I had
nothing to lose.

'Can you put me forward for Harrods?' I asked Dora, when
I went to see her.

She stared at me in surprise. 'But I thought you were going
to Harvey Nichols.'

'The job has fallen through. Recruitment freeze. Can you
help me get an interview at Harrods?'

Dora said nothing as she picked some imaginary fluff off
her Cacharel.

'Harvey Nichols wanted me,' I said.

'Be that as it may, you haven't been the best student here.'

'And you haven't been the best tutor.'

Dora's cheeks flamed red as she looked at me. 'Why don't you try somewhere local?' she said.

In the end, I'd got an interview at Harrods by applying directly but they'd turned me down. As had Waitrose, John Lewis and Marks & Spencer. No one seemed to want to give me a job and I knew that Estée Lauder was my last hope when I walked in to see them about a trainee scheme.

The air was heavy with the smell of Youth Dew as the recruitment officer smiled at me, her face so perfectly made up she resembled a waxwork doll. 'So why do you want to work for Estée Lauder?' she said.

'Why do I want the job?' I replied, asking myself the question more than the interviewer.

There was a moment of silence. 'Because I really love make-up?'

The woman's smile faltered for just a second.

Lord John jumper

'Please, Mary,' John says, as I sob in the passenger seat beside him. 'Please, please, don't cry.'

'But I don't understand. I know you love me. I know you do.'

'I don't know if I do any more.'

'But you do.'

'It's too hard having a long-distance relationship. York is

miles away. And I feel like I have to come back to see you each weekend. I can't do it.'

'But you promised me it would be fine when you got the job!'

'I know I did. I thought it would be. But it's not.'

'If we love each other, then nothing matters, does it? We can make it work.'

'We can't. We've been arguing ever since I moved. It's just not making either one of us happy any more.'

'But it is! I'm happy. Don't you see, John? We're going to marry, have children, have a family. We've talked about it.'

'Yes. We have. But I don't feel that way any more.'

Panic washes over me as I look at John. He is light, his home a haven. His dad John is a train driver and his mum Gladys invites me for Sunday lunches with all the family. They breed miniature dachshunds. Their world feels safe and familiar. I am part of it. John is part of mine.

We are sitting in the car outside Tish's flat. I am living in her and Phil's spare room now that I have left Sheila and Harry's. My sister is getting married in two months and I am going to be a bridesmaid. John is going to be there with me. We will get married one day too.

Sitting beside me, John starts to cry as he looks at me. 'I'm so sorry, Mary,' he says. 'I'm just so sorry.'

Phil finds me crumpled in a heap on the doorstep after I knock on the front door. As he takes me inside, Joe and Tish stare at me in confusion.

'I just don't understand,' I sob. 'I know we've been arguing a bit but I know he loves me too. I'm sure of it. I am.'

Tish cries too as Joe and Phil sit either side of me on the sofa. They all love John. He is part of our team. As Hurricane Higgins hits snooker balls into pockets on the TV, Joe and Phil each take one of my hands in theirs. For the next month, I go to bed wearing a Lord John jumper – one of John's favourites which he left at Tish's the last time he came over. As I try to sleep surrounded by his familiar smell, I feel my heart breaking in a way it hasn't since Mum died.

Yale key

'How are you, Mary?' Dad asks.

I've got a Saturday job at Clements as a floater. I go from department to department, depending on where I'm needed, and it's earning me just about enough to get by. I can't pay my way properly with the people I'm living with but they understand. It's about all I can do to eke out my Saturday wage for bus fares and other essentials. I don't see Dad too often now. He doesn't work every weekend at Clements and is either in his office or sitting in the management canteen if he does come in.

'Isn't he a lovely man, your father?' the other sales girls say, when they discover I'm Sam's daughter. 'Such a gentleman. So kind.'

I try to avoid him. But every so often he brings some post for me to give to Joe or Tish if he doesn't have time to drop it off at Clipso.

'I'm okay,' I say.

'And how's college?'

'Okay.'

'Joe said you had a job?'

'It fell through.'

'And John?

'We've finished.'

Surprise flickers across Dad's face. 'I'm sorry to hear that.'

I look around as I shift from foot to foot. 'I'd better be getting back. I'm in Menswear today.'

I want to turn and fling myself at Dad as I walk away. I want to run to him as I did when I was a child, slip my hand into his and feel safe because I'm more afraid now than I ever have been: no home, no money, no job, no John.

But I will not give Dad the satisfaction of asking for help, just as I won't beg Dora. Something has hardened inside me. I have only myself to rely on. If I don't get myself out of this mess then no one else will. I can't keep begging favours from people and asking for handouts.

Breaking and entering is the answer. Knowing that Dora keeps the key to her office tucked on top of the doorframe when she goes for lunch each day, I ask Suzanne to stay on watch in the corridor while I steal the key, let myself into Dora's office and use her phone to ring the Harrods personnel department. The young man at the other end listens patiently as I explain that I need another interview. They got it wrong. I'm perfect for Harrods. I'll work hard. I have ideas. I'll do a good job.

'But all our positions are filled,' he told me. 'I do not have a job to offer you.'

'Are you sure?'

'Completely sure, Miss Newton.'

'A hundred per cent sure? Harvey Nichols offered me a job. I think you would, too, if you gave me another chance.'

'I'm sorry but we don't have a vacancy for a junior display assistant. There is really nothing I can do to help.'

I cannot give up. I start to steal the key to Dora's office each lunchtime. As my hand closes around it at twelve thirty every day, my heart beats like a drum because I know this is my final chance to get the job I want.

'Any vacancies yet?' I ask the man on a Monday.

'No, Miss Newton.'

'Anyone turned down a job?' I say on a Tuesday.

'No, Miss Newton.'

'Are you sure there isn't a job for me?' I say on a Wednesday.

'No. But if one becomes available then I'll be sure to let you know.'

'Just checking that no one has dropped out?' I ask on a Thursday.

'No. No one has dropped out.'

I can hear him laughing.

'It's a personal call,' I tell the Harrods telephonist on a Friday, to avoid being cut off.

It takes weeks to make him crack. But three days after leaving Cassio, I go up to Harrods for another interview. Putting on my best Miss Selfridge pencil skirt, a white shirt and stilettos, I stuff my portfolio with half of Suzanne's work and walk through the store doors. By the time I get home, there is a message waiting for me. I have been offered a job.

Mink, macaroons and alligators

Some came to buy a mink coat or a bottle of champagne to drink with a box of rainbow-coloured macaroons. Others were looking for a bale of the finest Egyptian cotton towels or diamonds that would drip from their ears for years to come. There were lights handcrafted by artisans in Venice, antique Indian art and carpets woven around the world; monogrammed stationery, silver cutlery and pedigree puppies. Harrods was the store where almost anything was possible.

Covering four and a half acres, it stretched across seven floors and underground into a warren of rooms that connected to the huge depository building on Trevor Square. There were carpenters and chocolate-makers, waiters and seamstresses, liveried liftmen and sales staff working either on the shop floor or behind the scenes for more than three hundred departments – all of which had plinths, cabinets and internal windows that needed to be designed and styled by the sixty-strong display team. The jewel in Harrods's crown was the seventy-two ground-floor windows facing onto the streets of one of London's most exclusive neighbourhoods. In them, dreams became reality and customers were enticed over the threshold into the magic kingdom.

The back windows that faced onto Basil Street were filled with a mix of products from home, beauty, fine wine, childrenswear and books to cookshop, accessories and food while menswear was displayed in those along the side of the building in Hans Crescent. The front windows facing onto Brompton Road boasted big-ticket furniture items and bridalwear but were mainly designed around the most expensive designer women's fashion, jewellery and accessories because fashion was one of Harrods's main draws.

Selfridges, Harvey Nichols and Liberty had yet to be reinvented as fashion destinations and the high-street revolution was a distant dream. Everyone, from international jet-setters in search of glamour to tourists who wanted a glimpse of it, came to Harrods. Silk, satin and velvet from the big French and Italian houses, like Dior, Valentino and Yves Saint Laurent, were taken off shelves and out of boxes to be put at the centre of fantastical scenes, alongside pieces by classic British designers, including Janice Wainright and Jean Muir, and newer Italian talents, like Armani and Cerruti.

Windows, windows, windows, I silently intoned, when I walked into Harrods for my first day, knowing that Danielle had been assigned to the ground-floor beauty team.

'Second floor, home department,' my new boss John McKittrick told me.

My heart sank.

The Face magazine

A month later I was sitting with my new colleagues on the back-windows team after finding out they needed a junior and going straight to see Mr McKittrick.

'I'd like to transfer,' I said, when I walked into his office.

With a long face, overhung jaw and slightly droopy air, Mr McKittrick resembled a camel and was constantly orange because of too much time spent on a sunbed in Marbella. His eyes flicked up towards me as he sat at his desk. 'You're on the second floor!'

'I know. But they need someone on the back windows. I got my best college marks for windows. I'd really like to learn more about them.'

'It's not normally how we allocate roles,' Mr McKittrick said, as he shuffled some papers. 'But it's true. They do need a junior.'

'I'm a junior!'

He sighed. 'I know you are, Mary.'

'And I'd love to get the chance.'

'All right, then. But if it doesn't work out we'll have to transfer you to another floor.'

I made sure that didn't happen. Ripping up floor coverings, unscrewing light bulbs and returning products to their departments, I dismantled windows as the rest of the team prepared to fill them again. Caroline, the display manager for back windows, was strongest at bold interior styling – transforming products by draping fabrics or grouping lights without so much as a backward glance as she chatted to me about which pub or club she'd been to the night before. Her deputy, Elaine, the senior dresser, was the perfect foil: good on the tiny details that made windows look polished. Fiona and Roger, the dressers who made up the team, assisted them both and I was the junior at the bottom of the pile.

Once the windows had been emptied and Caroline's designs for new displays signed off by Mr McKittrick, I'd follow whoever I was helping around the store as they picked new products. Steaming and ironing clothes in the studio, collecting boxes of bulbs from the store, cutting up felt to make floor coverings or digging through the huge stock of general props – everything from bunches of plastic grapes and lamps, to cut-outs of moons and suns or wood lettering – I did anything that was asked of me and quickly learned about the store as I went from department to department.

Our titular bosses were Mr McKittrick and his deputy Lou Desmond, a small man with the unfortunate habit of licking his closed fist before dabbing it on a face that always seemed to be overheating.

'Never forget we're selling a dream!' Mr Desmond would singsong, at the end of each morning's briefing as he pawed his face – even though his squealing, high-pitched commands during the other seven hours and fifty minutes of the working day had earned him the nickname Desdemoaner.

But Mr McKittrick and Mr Desmond were merely bit players as far as the windows teams were concerned. For us, there was really only one person in control: Berge, the head of fashion and queen of the store. Tall, dark and thin as a whippet, he looked like a cross between Rudolf Nureyev and Freddie Mercury without the buck teeth. With a moustache clipped pristinely above his top lip, Berge favoured mohair jumpers worn with such closely cut lilac or lemon trousers we all knew on which side he dressed and spoke in a lisping drawl that had a hint of his Armenian background when it was raised to concrete-digger level.

'*Theees* is fucking *sheeeet*!' he'd yell as assistants trailed in his wake, flailing around him as he shot out commands. 'Do eet again!'

The rest of the time, Berge spoke hardly a word. You'd never find him laughing at a joke or sniping a witty comment at another dresser. While the rest of us laughed, gossiped and argued together in the studio, Berge was always serious, a man apart with two ways of being: stalking around the ground floor with his eyes narrowed or sitting with the fashion buyers in the canteen – women so sleek and groomed they looked like a flock of swans – with his eyes narrowed. He didn't muck around, he wasn't bitchy: he was driven, and part of his job as head of fashion was to create the most beautiful windows I'd ever seen.

Even a novice like me could see that Berge had extraordinary talent. Staring at his windows, I'd wonder not just at the scale of his imagination in designing the displays but his technical detail: skirt hems that looked as if they were fluttering in the wind, silk and velvet scarves pinned so that the luxury of the fabric was revealed in a single shadow falling on a tuck.

The front-windows team worked with him to create this and was made up of men whose moustaches were so luxuriant they often came round the corner before they did. Clad in skin-tight denim and reeking of aftershave, they wore shirts with enough buttons open to reveal at least a large portion of their hairy chests if not a hint of their navel. Rumour had it that some stuffed socks down their jeans in order to up the ante even further.

You could tell the straight ones by the way they dressed. Peter Harvey, who was on the front windows and mainly styled interiors, was instantly recognizable by his checked shirts, cords and leather jacket. It was all in the best possible taste but a very different look – he still had the hairy chest but hid most of it bar a few curls, thanks to the impeccably white Hanes Ts he wore underneath his shirts. Keith Mowser, who ran the side windows, had a beard, a twinkle in his eyes for the ladies and favoured elephant cords and cashmere jumpers. His assistant, Jill, had such long blonde hair that we nick-named her Joyce McKinney, even though she'd never made a sex slave of anyone. Their junior was a guy called Sam, who dressed like a Teddy Boy and had been at Cassio with me.

Occasionally I was asked to assist in other windows but the back ones felt like home. I enjoyed the breadth of product they contained, which meant that I was learning about the whole store. But mostly I treasured my friendship with Caroline, Elaine, Fiona and Roger. It was a lifeline. They had no idea just how much I needed them and I don't think I did either.

The five of us are sitting now in one of the back windows that we're supposed to be restyling. The blinds are down and passers-by on the street outside will see a hand-painted sign in the window, saying, 'Pardon our appearance while we dress our windows.' But instead of working, we are staring at Siouxsie Sioux on the cover of this month's *Face*.

I've been almost as addicted to the magazine since it was

launched a few months ago as I am to Siouxsie: the way she writhes around the stage with the air of a woman so completely in control of herself, her music and everyone around her. I've been to see her and the Clash and the Pretenders, and how anyone can bear to hear Abba bleating on about the winner taking it all is still beyond me.

Siouxsie is wearing black-and-white tartan and a huge lace collar. Her hair is cut in her trademark spiky black crop that matches her thickly pencilled eyebrows. The only colour on the page is the magazine's logo, a couple of headlines and Siouxsie's bright red lips.

She is so beyond cool.

'Do you think I should cut off my hair like Siouxsie?' Fiona says.

'Would you really do that?' Roger squeaks.

In his stone-washed jeans and loafers, Roger's idea of musical heaven is Sylvester singing 'You Make Me Feel (Mighty Real)'.

'Yes, I would,' says Fiona 'I'm bored of my hair. I want to do something different.'

We stare at the mass of dark curls tumbling down Fiona's back.

'You've gotta do it!' I shriek.

'When?'

'Tonight! If you think too much you'll lose your nerve.'

'Right. I will. And I'm going to save up for some new leather trousers too.'

We all sigh in admiration. Fiona is going to get a Siouxsie cut. It's like Kate Bush has announced she's going punk.

N. Peal cashmere socks

There are two types of mannequin: the ones that wear shoes and the ones that don't. Adel Rootstein mannequins wear shoes and are held in place with fine wire that's almost invisible when it is pinned to their waist and tacked to the floor to keep them upright. These are the willowy blondes or brunettes decked in designer clothes and shoes that you see in the front windows of stores.

Cheaper mannequins are held in place by spigots – large metal screws embedded in the round or square bases they stand on and fit into holes in the mannequins' feet. We used these on the back windows and cut holes in tights and socks to get the spigot through because the mannequins had to have their feet covered.

Buyers were constantly sighing when I went to sign out products to use in our displays.

'We had a Pucci scarf come back with pin marks last week,' they would snap at me. 'And a belt with a scuff. We can't sell those products now, you know. We'll have to sign them off as damaged.'

As the buyers glared at me, I'd solemnly promise that no harm would come to whatever I was borrowing for our display. Mostly that was true. The only things that were regularly damaged were the tights and socks. But they had to be cut for the spigots.

Mysteriously, though, the male mannequins standing at

the centrepiece of a back-window tableau celebrating the joys of golf or small leather goods never wore socks from the cheaper end of Harrods's sock range. Instead they always had the most beautiful N. Peal cashmere on their feet that had to be written off as damaged against the display department's budget. They should have been put into a staff sale. Instead they usually ended up on our feet.

Mannequins deserve well-shod feet. It was the first important lesson I learned at Harrods.

Sobranie cigarettes

'Where did you go trolling off to last night, then?' the dresser sharing the café table with us says to his friend.

'I met a crimper and couldn't resist him.'

My colleagues had been born when homosexuality was still a crime and some of the older ones still threaded Polari – the language that gay men had once used to communicate secretly – through their conversations. I'd never heard it until I got to Harrods where I listened to men use it to talk about the morning after the night before as I sat in the Arco café in Hans Crescent. The unofficial Harrods staff room, the Arco was the place where gossip was constantly exchanged over mugs of tea in a fug of steam, cigarette smoke and the smell of fat. And soon I'd learned enough Polari to understand tales of nightclubs, bars and bondage nights, break-ups, make-ups and everything in between.

As they swapped stories of where they had been and with whom, I learned that the men I worked with couldn't get enough of the new nightclub Heaven that had opened on the old site of Global Village, which I'd once visited with my brothers. Heaven had brought gay men out of basement clubs into the mainstream and they were celebrating.

'Why is there no love in my life?' Roger sighs, as we sit in the Arco deciding what to order. 'I just don't know what I'm doing wrong.'

We do. Roger keeps insisting he's straight.

Luigi walks past our table in his waiter's uniform: a red shirt, black bow tie and black trousers.

'"One day I'll fly *awaaaay*,"' he sings breathily, as he stops and bends down towards Caroline. Luigi loves to hear himself sing.

'"Leeve all theees to yesserdayyyyyy."'

Caroline looks at him blankly. 'Can we get five mugs of tea and three rounds of toast, please?'

Luigi's face falls. '"What more could your loff to do meeeee?"' he whispers plaintively, then shuffles off, Caroline following him to the counter.

'So are we going to Borshtch N Tears on Friday?' says Elaine. 'It's payday. Shall we treat ourselves?'

Usually we save our money for drinks in the Metro Wine Bar or a cheap meal in Stockpot. But when we're feeling a bit flush, a couple of days after being paid, we go to proper restaurants with things like white napkins, breadbaskets and candles. I know I shouldn't treat myself but can't resist a night out, even though I'm constantly worried about money.

Having left Tish's and moved back to Sheila and Harry's for a couple of months, I'm now staying with Aunty Mary and Uncle Jim in Tufnell Park because it's closer to Harrods.

Going from place to place, always aware of relying on people for a roof over my head in already crowded homes, I spend weekends in Watford because then I'm not under anyone's feet. I also get to see Cathy, Ruth, Jean, Joe and Tish. Joe is still at Clipso, and Tish is now working as a nurse at UCH but living in Watford so they're always around. Michael and Lawrence are not in Watford as much because Michael often travels for work and Lawrence is busy at weekends with his friends from the police cadets. I still wonder if he'll actually want to be a police officer when he turns eighteen and starts training for real. Maybe he'll suddenly realize what it all means. But for now at least he seems happy enough.

I know I should get my own place but the thought of living alone fills me with dread. It took me months to get used to not having Tish on the bottom bunk every night in Windsor Road when she started her nursing course – and I had two brothers and a dad lying only a few feet away. The thought of being by myself makes me shudder.

I can hardly afford to get somewhere of my own either on the amount I earn. I'm continually dodging fares on the Underground and buying food that's discounted because it's near the end of its shelf life as I try to save money. Fashion and music are the only things I want to spend anything on. I save up for weeks before going to buy a T-shirt at Rock-A-Cha in Kensington Market, Take Six on the King's Road or PX in Covent Garden. I squirrel away any spare money I have to buy records by artists like Joy Division, Talking Heads and Dexys Midnight Runners. Working-class kids are breaking the charts with music featuring everything from synthesizers to brass and strings.

'Did you see Berge this morning?' Fiona asks. 'I thought he was going to strangle Tracy.'

'What had she done wrong?'

'I don't know. Probably missed a speck of dust when she vacuumed the window.'

'Good job he didn't catch you, Mary!'

I smile at Fiona. 'Never. It was a fail-safe plan.'

A few days before, the after-effects of one too many the night before had caught me up when we were redoing a window. The blinds were down and Caroline could see that I was struggling. 'Have a quick nap,' she said.

So I'd got a Frette throw – because by now I'd started to learn just how much softness money could buy you at the luxury end of linens – and lain down with the hum of shoppers passing by outside, hidden from view as Caroline screwed shut the panel giving access to the back of the window. Twenty minutes later she'd woken me up.

'I've got us a treat!' she says, as she comes back to the table with our mugs of tea. 'Toast is just coming.'

Reaching into her bag, she pulls out a packet of Sobranie. Snapping back in our seats like Pavlovian dogs, we look nonchalantly at the box. Sobranies aren't kids' fags. They're for sophisticated adults, the kind of people who go to San Lorenzo every day of the week. I hardly smoke but make an exception for Sobranie.

'What colour do you want?' Caroline asks, as we gaze at the neat row of green, yellow, pink and lilac cigarettes nestling in the box.

'Yellow maybe?' says Fiona.

'Green?' I wonder.

'Bags the pink one!' Roger shrieks.

The eyes of the queens sitting beside us slide wordlessly towards him.

Blitz kids

I don't think I've ever spent so much time getting ready for a night out. And that's saying something.

But Roger, Fiona and I have to look our best to get past the bloke on the door of the Blitz club. His name is Steve Strange and he's the scariest twenty-one-year-old in London. We've got in the few times we've come, but you can never be sure with Steve. Stalking up and down outside the door, he gazes at people before either showing them inside with a nod or turning them away.

'Take a look, love,' he says to a woman in front of us. His lip curls with disgust as he holds up a mirror in front of her. 'Would you let yourself in?' he snaps.

The woman, who is wearing a wetsuit and flippers, disappears into the night without another word.

Recession, high unemployment and strikes – everything bleak about life in 1980 – is forgotten inside the Blitz as teenagers and twenty-somethings create looks that owe more to the pages of story books than real life. Art students, musicians, fashion designers, hairdressers and shop assistants parade in a whirl of fur, leather, Spandex, leopard and everything in between, faces painted like masks and hair teased into clouds.

David Bowie is their muse and has even dropped in to see what is happening here, the buzz that Steve and DJ Rusty Egan have created with friends, including Boy George, Stephen Jones, Midge Ure and the Kemp brothers. One day soon this look will be labelled New Romantic. For now, all I know is that I will die a thousand deaths if I don't get over the threshold of the club.

A night at the Blitz takes weeks of preparation. Each time we come, Fiona, Roger and I spend hours rooting through the studio and prop cupboard looking for anything that has been written off as damaged that we might be able to customize. Tonight I've paired green army trousers and a white shirt with a purple felt conical hat that Roger decked with blue netting. My eyes glitter with silver and my mouth is streaked with a slash of bright red. Fiona is wearing a tutu, with black fishnets and red glitter shoes, and her hair is so backcombed she'll have to wash it at least a dozen times to straighten it out. Roger, meanwhile, is in a shirt that we fashioned out of bubble wrap and stapled onto him. He's also wearing a black silk tie and full make-up. Wear anything like this anywhere other than the Blitz and you might be beaten up. But here anything is possible.

Nerves fill me as we get nearer to Steve. I wonder what we'll find inside the Blitz tonight: wood nymphs, queens wearing crowns, priests, pirates or space cadets maybe, all dancing in a club that's decked out with war memorabilia as past and future collide.

'There is no way he's turning us away,' Fiona hisses, as we move up the queue. 'No way. I haven't eaten lunch for a week to pay for tonight.'

And then there he is in front of us.

Steve looks us up and down before dropping his eyes to the ground. His face is painted white and his eyes are so kohled I'm not sure he'll be able to see a thing.

'In you go,' he says at last.

If Roger moves any quicker, I swear the bubble wrap will rip.

Sinclair ZX80

Our breath trails in clouds around us. It's a cold winter's night and we're standing in front of the back windows. Christmas was unveiled earlier tonight and shoppers jostled to get a glimpse of the most luxurious displays of the year. Now it's past eleven and the street is quiet. Caroline, Elaine, Fiona, Roger and I have stopped for one last look on the way home from the pub.

The front and side windows are full of stories – fairies, princesses and knights dressed in the latest couture and most expensive accessories. Ours are dressed with everything else the store has to offer. Food and china, furniture, luggage and textiles brought together in scenes of a fantasy home prepared for a magical Christmas. Games are at the centre of Caroline's design, every kind that you can imagine: hand-tooled leather chess and backgammon sets stacked alongside dominoes made of walnut and elm; board games like Risk and Monopoly, with the red, blue, yellow and green lights of Simon games winking beside them. There is a fireplace stacked with logs and giant hand-painted baubles hanging from the ceiling. Striped stockings are suspended along the mantelpiece, chocolate and crystallized fruits tumble out of boxes and a Christmas tree laden with lights stands in a corner. It's what every child dreams of waking up to find on Christmas morning.

'What on earth do you do with it?' Fiona had exclaimed, when she opened a box as we dressed the windows.

Sitting in the bottom was a Sinclair ZX80 computer – one of the latest in electronics that would form the centrepiece of our windows. A white plastic square with a blue keyboard, the Sinclair was billed as the first affordable home computer that you connected to your TV and used to play games like Space Invaders and Pacman. Beside the ZX80 were boxes with 'Atari' written on them and smaller packages too: tiny plastic and glass games with a screen featuring a black stick figure that tossed around balls. They were called Game & Watches. It all looked like something out of *Star Trek*.

'I haven't got a clue,' I'd said to Fiona. 'And why anyone would want to sit at home in front of a big white box instead of going to a video arcade with their mates is beyond me.'

I looked solemnly at her.

'It'll never catch on,' I said.

An unexpected visit

I picked up the phone and dialled Mr McKittrick's number. My hands shook slightly as I waited to be put through to him.

It was a few days after the Christmas windows had been unveiled and I'd gone to see Tish the night before after work. But when I'd got to her flat, I'd found Rebecca waiting outside in the dark.

'Is your sister here?' she'd asked.

'She'll be back soon.'

'I need to talk to you both.'

'What about?'

Rebecca's face crumpled in the orange glow of the street-lights. 'Your father is dead.'

Something swooped down inside me just as it had when Mum died. That moment of going over a cliff and plunging downwards. I did not understand. 'What do you mean? Dad's not ill.'

'A heart attack. In his office. Can I come in and wait for your sister? I'd like to tell her the news. I've lost him and we've only been married nine months.'

Anger snapped as I looked at Rebecca dabbing her nose with a handkerchief, lost in her own sadness, entirely unaware of ours. 'I'll do it,' I said. 'We'll ring you tomorrow about the arrangements.'

Unlocking the front door, I left Rebecca standing outside as I walked into the flat.

'Mr McKittrick?' I said now, as I heard him pick up the phone. 'It's Mary Newton. I can't come in today. My father has died.'

He was silent for just a moment too long, and the familiar unease of a person trying to find the right words rushed back to me.

'I'm so sorry, Mary,' Mr McKittrick said. 'That's dreadful.'

Dreadful. The word stuck in my mind as I put down the phone. Mr McKittrick was right. But, in so many ways, Dad had been lost to us long before.

A funeral

For a man who'd spent his childhood in the Protestant Church, was married and raised children in the Catholic before a late conversion to Seventh Day Adventism, my father's funeral was an appropriately mixed affair when it came to religious influences. After a service in a nondescript non-denominational church, we went to North Watford cemetery where Dad was buried next to Mum as his very much alive second wife wept beside them.

It had been a battle to get him there. When the five of us had gone to discuss arrangements with Rebecca, she had looked at us in surprise after Michael had mentioned the funeral at St Helen's and burial beside Mum in our local cemetery.

'But he's my husband now,' Rebecca had said. 'And I want him to be buried in my church.'

'He bought the plot after Mum died,' Michael replied. 'It's beside hers. They were married for twenty-four years.'

'I know. But that was before we met and he grew to share my faith.'

We'd gone straight to see Father Bussey.

'She can't do this, can she?' Joe had exclaimed. 'It's not what Dad would have wanted. We know it isn't.'

Father Bussey had agreed to go and see Rebecca with us the following day to try to reason with her. Anger had once again boiled up inside me as he gently explained how important it was for us that our parents were buried together.

'I'm really not sure it's what Sam would have wanted,' Rebecca said.

In the end she had reluctantly agreed to let us bury Dad beside Mum. But Rebecca had held fast to having the service in a non-denominational church. Her priest spoke and Father Bussey said a few words. It was a religious no man's land.

I thought of Mum as Father Bussey talked. I thought of what she would say and how she would feel if she knew what she'd worked so hard to create had disappeared. The family that Mum would have recognized was no more. It was finally being laid to rest with Dad. Sitting with Michael, Joe, Tish, Phil and Lawrence, I felt grief mix with numbness inside me.

Don, Sadie, Jean, Ruth, Cathy, Harry and Sheila were there, as well as colleagues and other friends. But it felt like a pitiful affair as Rebecca cried softly on her pew and tears slid unnoticed down my cheeks.

We'd asked Rebecca for a couple of things – photos, a few of Mum's favourite knick-knacks and Dad's watch because we all knew he wanted Joe to have it. None of it was worth anything. We just wanted to save a few bits of our past for the future. I kept thinking of the bedspread covered with black Scottie dogs that Mum had bought me as a child. Where was it? I didn't know why but I ached for it. What had Dad done with it when he'd packed up the house?

'The solicitor will deal with it all,' Rebecca kept saying, in response to our questions. 'Your father got rid of most things.'

The solicitor told us just before the funeral that Dad had left everything to Rebecca. Money and every possession he'd ever owned. Now it was just the five of us.

Hovis crumpets

It is a week since I moved into my own place a couple of weeks after Dad's funeral. It's the silence that gets me most. When Michael walked me home a few days ago, after I'd had dinner with him and his girlfriend, Ros, who lives just around the corner, I'd sobbed as he said goodbye.

'Everything will be okay,' my brother told me, as we hugged.

But each time I unlock the door to my bedsit in Manor

House, I just want to cry. With lino on the floor and the smell of damp in the air, it has an electricity meter that needs to be repeatedly stuffed with coins that I am always either forgetting or cannot afford. The bathroom down the corridor has plugholes constantly clogged with other people's hair and is so freezing I almost can't bring myself to use it.

The house is on several floors and at night I hear people running up and down the stairs, laughing and joking as they come in or go out. But when I get home from Harrods, the only thing I can bring myself to do is heat up a can of soup on the Baby Belling and get into bed. It's November, freezing cold, and as I lie in the dark because the bloody meter has usually run out, I switch on the radio and listen to anything that's on just to hear the sound of voices filling the room. The silence is heavy. Almost like a weight. While the rest of the country has been gripped by finding out who shot JR, I've lain in bed listening to Radio 1. 'Flash' by Queen is at number one, and if I've heard it once I've heard it a thousand times.

At least I'm warm in bed. John's mum, Gladys, has given me some purple flowered sheets and a duvet. She'd heard that I was moving and knew I didn't have anything. I've never had a duvet before. John dropped it round to me with his dad and I'd stared hopefully at him, as I always do when I see him. He'd looked at me awkwardly before leaving again. We see each other quite often now but he's told me that we can only ever be friends. And while I have new boyfriends, they never last long because I cannot stop myself hoping that one day John will change his mind.

My eyes filled with tears yesterday when Simon Bates played 'Without You' by Nilsson. *Our Tune* has only been on a few months but already everyone in the Harrods studio is addicted to the stories of lost and thwarted love. Years ago, I'd played 'Without You' over and over on a jukebox in a French youth hostel. I was on a school trip with St Joan's and had always imagined my first time abroad would be far more exotic than forty-eight hours in a rainy town in Normandy.

But I'd never really understood the words properly until I heard it as I ironed shirts in the studio. I didn't dare cry at work but realized a few days later that I needn't have worried. The day after John Lennon was murdered, I walked into the studio to find it lit by hundreds of candles and everyone sobbing as they drank wine and remembered him.

But today I am not going to cry. Today I am going to smile and pretend everything is fine because Tish is coming to see me. She cried when she dropped me off here with my two suitcases, the kettle and the toaster she and Phil had bought me. Tish worries that I can't cope on my own but I keep telling her that I can. I've been looking after other people for a long time so I must be able to do the same for myself. I can't keep running back to her.

It's my first weekend in my flat and I have forced myself not to go back to Watford. So this morning I took my washing to a local launderette instead of taking it to Tish's, then went to see Ros for brunch. Her flat is so cosy that she almost has to drag me off the sofa when it's time to leave.

I can't stop thinking of Dad. I pray that God will forgive

him for what he did. I don't want him to be punished for choosing Rebecca over us. I want him to be in Heaven with Mum where he should be. I want them to be together. I whisper the words of my prayers as I lie in bed.

There is a knock on the door and I run to open it. Tish is standing outside looking pale. I gather her up in a hug. 'Step this way,' I say, as I usher her inside.

Tish glances around the room. Her face falls even further.

'I couldn't bake a cake,' I say brightly. 'But look what I got for our tea!' I hold up a packet of crumpets. 'And I've got butter as well. Two packets.'

Tish gives me a smile. I smile back. Later we will talk about Dad. Why he did what he did. Still not understanding it. But we know the pain will gradually soften. We have learned this before.

Pierrot dolls and Baileys

The weeks in the run-up to Christmas are like no other in the retail year. It starts quietly enough: people slowly browse the almost empty Christmas department and organized women tick off lists of soap, socks, jumpers, games, books and a bottle of perfume for their mothers. Then everything spirals into complete and utter chaos.

Harassed mothers push screaming toddlers around in buggies as they fling whatever they can grab into a basket. White-faced men sprint towards the lingerie department to buy something special enough to make their wives smile for a moment before she disappears under a mountain of Brussels sprout peelings on Christmas morning. Lovers looking for a unique gift wrestle their way along miles of the store's walkways in the search for something perfect.

It is as if the world is preparing for a nuclear attack and the people working in retail are in charge of filling the bunkers. But then comes the magical moment around four o'clock on Christmas Eve when you realize there are just a few more hours to go. Tomorrow there will be one day of peace to savour before the madness starts again with the sales.

I'd like to say I was drunk with relief by late afternoon on my first Christmas Eve at Harrods. Instead I've drunk a large portion of a bottle of Baileys followed by a couple of brandy chasers. I am part of a skeleton windows team whose job it is to retrieve items from windows if people want to buy them, then fill the gap that has been left. I am sitting with Roger and Caroline in a small cupboard to the right of door one. It is called 'the front box' and about an hour ago we decided to celebrate with a drink and a mince pie.

But we've just had a call about a gold Dunhill lighter that is in a window filled with accessories behind small leather goods. It's needed urgently.

'We'll go,' I say to Caroline. 'But don't eat all the mince pies.'

I can hear Lord Mustard, the busker, playing outside as Roger and I step out of the front box to see shoppers stream inside the store.

'I can hardly see straight!' hisses Roger.

'Follow me!'

The window is filled with a wooden fireplace that we've had built. On and around it are stacked picture frames, lighters, wallets, crystal, glassware and fragrances. The colour theme is black, white and gold and we've finished off the window with a clutch of candles in the shape of Pierrot the clown. Shoppers are going mad for them.

After unscrewing the back panel, Roger holds onto it as I climb into the window. There isn't time to close the blinds. I see the lighter, force my eyes to focus properly and step towards it. But just as my hand closes around it, the back panel crashes into the window. It is a chain reaction of destruction as things fall one by one. Glasses sail through the air and a bottle smashes. Pierrot heads – decapitated by the force – go flying.

'It slipped out of my hands,' I hear Roger shrieking. 'It just slipped out!'

Shoppers stop on the other side of the glass as I stand frozen in the spotlights. They stare in horror. Christmas has been destroyed. There will be no peace for me the next day as I wonder if I will be sacked.

Ferragamo belt

My head is level with Berge's crotch. My eyes crawl past his belt buckle – Ferragamo – towards his flaring nostrils. I'm kneeling on the floor in front of a mannequin's leg. Her head looks uncannily like Joan Collins's. She is from Adel Rootstein's latest collection and I knocked off her leg as I tried to get her through the access panel into the window. If the leg is chipped it will have to be resprayed.

'Do you know how much eet cost?' Berge hisses, as his assistant glares at me. 'Peek it up!'

I scrabble on the floor but my hands have turned to jelly. Sweat beads on my upper lip. My heart thumps. Finally grabbing hold of the leg, I brandish it at Berge.

'Hold the feeking thing properly by its middle parts next time!'

Shoppers pass by as we stand in the beauty hall at the entrance to a front window. It's early January, and Roger and I escaped the Christmas fiasco by cobbling the display back together and withstanding a rocket from Mr McKittrick. Today I am assisting Berge with a window full of cruisewear. Apparently Harrods customers are preparing to board boats in the Caribbean and need lighter clothes for their holidays.

'Do I have to?' I'd said to Caroline, after Desdemoaner had told me at this morning's meeting that I was needed on the front windows.

I never enjoy going onto them. It's a busy day on front windows if you get to steam a dress whereas after seven months on the back ones I've been promoted to a dresser and am doing more and more. We've done displays hung with giant African masks to showcase travel and all its related products – furniture and leather goods from abroad, suitcases and trunks filled with rugs and chunky ethnic jewellery – and a window titled 'Table Top Dining on Four' that featured a mannequin wearing a table top around her midriff stacked with china and covered with a pleated cloth that doubled as a skirt.

Another showcased a replica of the Great Pyramid on a sand-covered floor to show off gold products, from gilt furniture to jewellery, shoes and gold-plated china, and we stood five willowy mannequins each holding the leads of fabric dogs whose coats matched their outfits – one with spots, another in checks, one in tweed, one in stripes and the last in tartan – in the windows to showcase haberdashery. A few designs had had to be ripped out after we'd installed them because they didn't work. You never knew how a drawing on paper would come to life but even the mistakes had taught me something.

I'd hoped I might get away with assisting Andrew or Peter on the front windows but instead I am at the mercy of Berge. So far this morning I have followed him around the store with two other assistants as he has picked a product, holding it up, letting it fall, feeling the fabric between his hands and scrutinizing it. One shade of yellow is too pale, another too sharp; a satin coat will look shiny under the lights; a velvet jacket is too heavy. Once everything is chosen, I take it down to the studio to press it before hanging the clothes on a rail outside the window.

Berge has already dressed two mannequins. There is just the last to do. I follow him into the window. It smells of paint and glue. Lights hanging from the ceiling illuminate a statuesque brunette lounging against a giant acid-green banana leaf. She is wearing pale lemon flared trousers and a peach silk shirt by Yves Saint Laurent, her entire right arm layered with gold bracelets. Another mannequin, legs astride and leaning against an azure blue wall, wears an Eres swimming costume and Oscar de la Renta sandals. Together they stand at the centre of a scene that melds haute couture with the tropics.

The floor has been painted pink and the front section nearest to the windowpane is covered with ripples of golden sand that I spent hours this morning vacuuming into the perfect position. Not a grain out of place. When Berge came to inspect what I'd done, his eyes had narrowed before he'd wordlessly climbed out of the window.

We are wearing just our socks to avoid marking the floors. I think of the hole in mine as I kneel down to place the mannequin's feet while the assistant carefully holds her body. She is going to wear a canary yellow lightweight woollen coat and a matching dress covered with bright pink flowers by Valentino. Berge will dress her, then we will wire her into position and he will do his final touches.

We hold the mannequin as Berge wriggles her dress over her head and puts on the coat. He slips pink Gianfranco Ferre sandals onto her feet. Not a crease can be made in the fabric or a single scuff on the leather. Berge's eyes narrow to slits as he concentrates. His movements are delicate, as if he's cradling a newborn. For Berge the product is a relic that cannot be defiled. He is economical and precise as he works. I hold my breath until black spots appear before my eyes, not daring to move. The air is heavy with the smell of his Halston aftershave.

We've already secured a loop of wire around the mannequin's waist and two longer sections trail down to the floor from underneath her dress. When Berge has finished dressing her, he stands back and I take the first piece of wire, pull it taut and hammer a nail into the floor to secure it near the mannequin's feet. I must be careful. I cannot chip the floor. The window is a fantasy, a dreamscape. It must be perfect.

I dread the moment when the assistant will let go of the mannequin to see if she is steady. If the wire is not in the perfect position, she might fall.

'Did you go out last night?' the assistant asks Berge, as I work.

'San Lorenzo,' he says, but I can hear in his voice that he doesn't want to talk.

His eyes bore into me as I move to the back of the mannequin and take the second piece of wire before nailing it into place. I think I've got the angle right. I've learned to wire mannequins pretty well by now but have never had to do it for Berge. I sit back on my heels as the assistant slowly lets go of the mannequin. She remains perfectly in position.

The assistant climbs out of the window as I stand up beside Berge and he pulls a roll of wire out of his pocket. In his right hand is a pair of tiny scissors. Reaching down into my tool belt, my fingers close around a box of pins. I cannot keep him waiting for a second if he needs anything. Berge kneels in front of the mannequin and snips one of the stitches in the hem of her skirt.

With just a few deft strokes, he threads the wire and bends the hem of the skirt before sitting back on his heels to inspect his work. The hem seems to flutter in the breeze. Light from overhead streams through banana leaves hanging from the ceiling. It bounces off the silk and makes it glow. With just a few tiny movements, Berge has made not just the fabric but the whole window come alive. The mannequins are stepping through a fantasy jungle as breezes whisper around them, and the chatter of monkeys echoes through the air. It is extraordinary.

'It is done,' Berge says, and steps out of the window.

Levi 501's

It was Valentine's night when I walked into the Hill Top Wine Bar in Pinner with Merry Smethurst. There were candles flickering everywhere and Rose Royce was playing on the speakers.

'One drink and then I'm going,' Merry muttered darkly, as we walked up to the bar.

We stared at the wine list. I honestly didn't know what any of it meant but everyone had taken to drinking buckets of wine in these bars so I'd joined in. We ordered our drinks before sitting at a table, surrounded by couples knocking back bottles of chardonnay before moving in for a snog.

'Coming out might not have been my best idea,' I finally admitted.

'No,' Merry replied. 'But we're here now so we might as well enjoy it. How's work?'

'I had a bit of an accident last week.'

'What did you do?'

'Dropped a crystal trophy worth thousands.'

'Mary!'

'I know. It had been stored in the Harrods safe for generations. McKittrick went mad. But it was a genuine accident. Fiona and I were trying to get it into a window and it was so heavy we dropped it. I'm usually so careful. I thought I was going to get sacked.'

'Will they dock your wages?'

'If they do, I'll be working at Harrods until I'm about ninety.'

Merry collapsed into giggles as the door opened and in walked a face from the past. I'd known Ian Atkins for years and he was with a guy I also knew from around Watford. With jet black curly hair, brown eyes and lashes as long as a cow's, he was incredibly good-looking. I'd always longed for him to ask me to dance at the New Penny when I was sixteen but he was a couple of years older and constantly had some pretty girl or other by his side. Then he'd disappeared and I'd only seen him occasionally. I'd heard he'd gone to university, which was unusual for kids from Watford, and apparently he was now working in Wales as a chemical engineer. He was wearing battered old Levi's and a white T-shirt. He must have been bloody freezing.

Ian walked up to our table. 'Hi, Mary!' he said, as he bent to give me a kiss. 'How are you?'

'Good.'

'Still at Harrods?'

'Just about.'

Merry giggled as Ian looked at me in confusion.

'I'll explain later,' I said. 'This is Merry.'

As Ian said hello, I turned towards his friend.

He smiled at me. His eyes were kind. Sexy too.

'I'm Mary,' I said. 'Joe Newton's sister.'

'Hi, Mary,' he replied. 'Good to meet you. I'm Graham. Graham Portas.'

The boxer

Celebrities loved Harrods. Mick Jagger, Rod Stewart, Gary Numan, Indira Gandhi, Margaret Thatcher, Sir Matt Busby, Bobby Charlton and George Best were among the ones I saw. Ingrid Bergman and Bette Davis were some of those I missed, and I thought of what Dad would have said if he'd known.

But while all these people caused a ripple of chat among the sales and display staff, there was one who caused more of a stir than most. A relative newcomer to notoriety, she'd walk into the store wearing a gathered skirt and white shirt looking like a thousand other well-born girls who came from a clique that had been dubbed the Sloane Rangers. Her name was Lady Diana Spencer.

'She's just walked in door seven!' David Seeley would yelp.

The boss of ground-floor display, David had a close-cut beard and earned himself the nickname David Squealy because this was what he did every time he laughed.

'She's on her way up to China. Bloody china department! Doesn't she need a lipstick?'

Diana never failed to cause excitement because her engagement to Prince Charles had just been announced and the whole country had come down with wedding fever. Then I stepped into a lift one day with Roger to find her standing in it alone. As we stood silently at either side of her, I held my breath and wondered if Roger was going to curtsy.

But there was only one well-known person with whom I ever exchanged any words. It happened as I climbed out of one of the back windows after dressing it. Access to the window was through one of the men's changing rooms and I'd asked a salesgirl to put up a sign saying that it wasn't in use while I was in the window. But as I got out, I found a man standing in the changing room in his boxer shorts. He was the biggest person I'd ever seen in my life.

'Welcome to the party!' Muhammad Ali said, as I stared at him.

Big Bertha

Christmas was hardly even a memory by the time we started preparing for Easter but there was really only one thing that could fill any display.

'We have to put Big Bertha in there,' Caroline had told me. 'Who's that?'

'The giant egg we make every year. She always has pride of place in our windows.'

I'd gone down into the warren of rooms under the store that housed stock and cold rooms, seamstresses and carpenters to find the chocolate-makers in a room filled with vats.

'Have one for yourself, why don't you?' the Irish ladies who stirred them said, as I ordered up Big Bertha and they offered me a chocolate.

There were boxes full of them everywhere.

'It will take us a week to make her!' the women had said. 'Now go on. Have another one.'

With a stomach full of chocolate, I headed off to find the men who built the props for our windows in the basement studio. We needed a miniature house painted in pastel colours to fill with eggs and confectionery. The carpenters, Eddie, Stan, Mick and Dave, would make it, Ted would paint it and Bob the ticket-maker would hand-paint the price signs in his beautiful calligraphy. Meanwhile there was Ernie, the fibreglass moulder, who made our props and was usually found light-headedly spraying them on the roof of the building, and one-finger George, who operated the freight lift with Dennis, who had only one leg.

Every time one of these men walked onto the shop floor, one of the buyers would bristle.

'Is this really us?' Sylvia would sigh, if I chatted for too long to someone wearing overalls. 'Think of the customers!'

'Keep your hat on, darlin'!' Ted, who looked like a male Mrs Tiggywinkle in dungarees, would boom before shuffling off back to the basement. 'Can't an old man have a flutter with a pretty gel?'

A couple of weeks after placing my orders for the painted house and Big Bertha, I went back down to the basement on the day that I was due to dress the window. With Ted's help, I took the props back upstairs and spent the next few hours carefully doing the display. Everyone else was busy and by now I was trusted to do displays alone so I filled the house with sugared almonds and hand-painted eggs. There was box after box of chocolates and tubes of rainbow-coloured jelly-beans. Turkish Delight, marshmallows and toffees were piled in glass jars. Big Bertha stood at the centre. I'd positioned the lights to bounce off her beautiful wrapping and I could see that Caroline had been right. Big Bertha was magnificent. All four feet of her.

Half an hour later, I got back from the canteen to find Caroline white-faced outside the window.

'You put the lights too close,' she said, before laughter exploded out of her.

Big Bertha's top had melted. She looked like a boiled egg ready to be eaten.

Chanel No 5

I'd seen Spandau Ballet at the Sundown Club, listened obsessively to Simple Minds on my new Walkman, in awe that I could now have music with me everywhere I went, and almost cried with frustration when Bucks Fizz got to number one wearing skater skirts that ripped off to reveal matching pants. But it was Vivienne Westwood's pirate look that dominated as Adam and the Ants topped the charts dressed in gold-braided jackets and war paint as they sang 'Stand And Deliver'.

Meanwhile I was channelling part Dexys Midnight Runners, part Hazel O'Connor. Strolling into Harrods wearing pin-striped baggy trousers with braces and a man's white shirt, I looked at least three inches taller, thanks to the blonde perm that I backcombed religiously each morning. But I'd had to smarten up. I'd been promoted.

Despite all my misdemeanours, I'd proved myself a good dresser and was regularly asked to assist Berge on the front windows. I'd even been allowed to accessorize a manne-quin in one of his windows, and eventually a day had come when he checked what I'd done and didn't change any-thing. He just narrowed his eyes, glared at me and left the window.

I was full of ideas but knew that I wouldn't be able to realize them all in the back-windows team. I wanted to be promoted from dresser to senior dresser but there wasn't a vacancy because Caroline, Elaine, Fiona and Roger weren't going any-where. The five of us were as close as ever and Elaine and I had now moved in with Fiona to a two-up-two-down cottage belonging to her uncle.

'It's damp, it's cold and it's cramped,' she'd said. 'Do you want to share?'

All of what she'd said was true – plus the fact that the house was miles out of town in Sudbury Hill and I had to share a bedroom with Elaine. But as we shopped and cooked together, watched *M*A*S*H* on the TV, drinking Fiona's home-brew beer, and I squeezed into my single bed with Graham on the nights when Elaine went away, I was happy.

Part of me didn't want to leave back windows and move onto another display team. But I knew it was time for me to do more so I applied for a senior dresser's job when it came up on the fourth floor. Its two biggest departments back then were Sports and Way In, and why someone had thought fit to house trainers, sports tops and balls on the Olympic Way on one side of the floor, and Harrods's younger more accessible fashion brands at Way In on the other was beyond me.

But while I wasn't interested in folding football shirts, I knew that Paul Falvey, the display manager, who looked like David Essex in cowboy boots, wasn't that interested in fashion. I applied for the job, got it and started off doing some sports display but quickly moved to working solely on Way In. Paul seemed as pleased as I was that he wouldn't have to cross the floor from sports to fashion.

My first task was to charm the head buyer, Barbara Deighton, a dynamic woman in her forties who oversaw Way In. She not only selected all the fashion but sold it, too, on the shop floor, and while her two assistant buyers, Judy and Geraldine, were into trends, Barbara favoured a classic look – perfect blonde blow-dry, immaculate make-up and skirt suits worn with court shoes. If she didn't like what I did, I'd never get anywhere.

I knew I could do a lot if I got the chance. Way In was full of younger, hipper brands but their display didn't reflect that. British designers like Ally Capellino, Betty Jackson, Sarah Dallas and Paul Howie hung on the rails alongside French Connection and international labels, including Jousse, Ciao and Michiko. It was innovative fashion at the lower end of the price range, and while classic designers needed classic display, I could see an opportunity at Way In to do something different.

As I headed into the Basil Street Wine Bar for my twenty-first birthday party, I knew I'd have to win Barbara over if I was to succeed. But I felt sure I could as I walked in on Graham's arm doused in a bottle of Chanel No 5 that he'd given me. Graham was a grown-up. He went to Belgium for business meetings, took me for Mai Thais at Coconut Grove in Mayfair and asked me on nights out with his clients. He was strong, capable and caring. He made me feel safe and we'd fallen quickly and easily in love.

But after almost a year at Harrods, I wanted my working life to change too. For now I had store displays to do for Way In – plinths, internal windows and cases around the department. What I hoped for, though, was a dedicated Way In window on the ground floor. It had never had one before. But I was determined to get Way In its own window. And Barbara was the key.

The Emmanuels

Tish and I have bought matching bubble skirts, are obsessed with 'Vienna' by Ultravox, 'Fade to Grey' by Visage, and I am on my first proper holiday abroad.

I've only ever been to France a couple of times for the weekend but Joe, Tish and Phil, Michael and Ros, Graham and I have caught the coach to a campsite in the South of France. We wanted Lawrence to come with us, too, but he's left the police and is working in Our Price so he couldn't get the time off. He'd enjoyed being a cadet but training for real had finally made him realize that the police force wasn't for him. He'd left Hendon, and although he wasn't sure what he'd do now, we were all relieved that at least he wasn't doing something he didn't enjoy.

And so the seven of us bake on the beach by day before sweltering in our tents at night. We drink red wine, eat cheese and I am still so obsessed with volumizing my hair that I've managed to take out all the lights on the campsite when Tish and I plugged in our hairdryers simultaneously.

'Quick, Mary, quick!' Tish shrieks, on a hot July morning a couple of hours after we started sunbathing. 'We're going to miss it!'

The sun beats down as we run across the campsite in our bikinis towards a bar. It's already stuffed with British people drinking pints as Tish and I push our way inside.

'We're never going to see a thing!' Tish cries, as we crane to see the TV that's sitting in a corner.

But we manage to get near enough to see a glass coach stopping at the bottom of the steps leading to St Paul's Cathedral. I watch as Diana Spencer begins to unfurl herself from inside. There is only one thing I want to see: the dress by Elizabeth and David Emmanuel. Unknowns until the future queen picked them to design for her.

Bit by bit, the dress is revealed. I can see frills, puffed sleeves and a veil as Diana and the dress emerge from the coach. It is a panoply of pearls, a sea of taffeta with a train that stretches for miles. It is a dress fit for a soon-to-be-princess. It is also really creased.

Berge must be having a stroke.

Love Hearts and tartan

Barbara Deighton might have been strict but she was also fair. I knuckled down, while she watched over me and learned that she could trust me. I filled the display areas with designs I knew she would like, constantly came up with ideas for new ways to showcase products, and we were soon united in our belief that Way In should get a dedicated ground-floor window.

Barbara recognized that it would only increase our profile and was a force to be reckoned with once she'd made up her mind. Not only was Barbara a head buyer and close to Berge, she was also married to the head buyer of men's accessories. Together they packed a punch when it came to persuading Mr McKittrick. We were soon allocated two windows at either side of a door on Hans Crescent, which had previously housed menswear. It wasn't Brompton Road but I couldn't ask for miracles.

But as Barbara and I had sat down to discuss the first display that I would design for the windows, I knew it was time to misbehave a little.

'We're thinking of an Arctic tundra,' she said. 'Pastel blue cashmere and grey silk in a snowy landscape. Something eye-catching but elegant.'

I sketched the window, got the design signed off by Mr McKittrick and set to work. I wasn't going to let anyone see that window until it was perfect, and I roped Ted and all the boys into making me props before heaving them into the windows.

'What's all this lot going to look like, then?' Ted asked, as his face went beetroot red with the effort. 'It's not the usual kind of thing they do 'ere, is it?'

Eventually the display was finished, I lifted the blinds and brought Barbara downstairs to see it. The mannequins were dressed in the cashmere and silk that she had requested but they weren't standing on an Arctic plain. Instead they were strutting down the streets of snowy New York. Lorry tyres were piled up in the corners of the window, there were black tyre tracks skidding through white snow and a row of mannequins' legs in tights just as I'd seen them do at Boy on the King's Road. The New York skyline twinkled behind it all on a backdrop I'd painted.

Barbara gazed at the window for a long time, then smiled. 'It's good,' she said. 'Very good.'

It was all the encouragement I needed. Soon those windows were full of everything from ripped tartan and thousands of Love Heart sweets that I stuck individually on the walls to bald mannequins wearing only sportswear and boxing gloves.

Joseph pumps

'How much did your shoes cost?' Mr McKittrick's secretary Jane asks me. 'Go and find something you want from the shoe department and I'll ask him to sign it off as a replacement.'

Someone had nicked my shoes when I took them off to get inside a window. They were nothing special. But I'm desperate for a pair of pale turquoise Joseph flats with a black wedge sole that I saw in the shoe department a week ago. The leather is like butter. They're unlike any shoes I've ever owned and probably never will. Working with fashion every day has only increased my appetite for it but I still survive on buying damaged stock at knock-down prices in the sales. I've bought a white Dunhill men's shirt, an Étienne Aigner leather jacket and a skin-tight Pucci dress.

But despite being promoted, my wage is still so low that I struggle all the time. Joe does my hair for free and I continually beg the beauty girls for samples. I buy cheap food and go to happy hours in bars. But money is a constant worry and I even got caught recently dodging fares on the Underground. Graham went mad and warned me that I could get a criminal record. I hadn't been prosecuted and he had paid my fine. Despite working hard, it frustrated me that money was always short.

My stolen shoes probably cost a tenner or something.

'They were seventy quid,' I say to Jane.

Soon I've slipped the Joseph pumps onto my feet.

Buffalo hat

Two things happened in quick succession when I'd been working at Way In for nearly a year. First I competed in Harrods' Good Housekeeping Awards – an annual battle of the display teams across all the store's departments about who could dress theirs the best – and won. I wasn't sure but I thought Berge might almost have cracked a smile when my name was announced. Soon after, Caroline handed in her notice at Harrods because she was going to work as an interior designer. It felt like the end of an era.

Elaine and Roger both applied for Caroline's job as display manager and Elaine should have got it, in the normal scheme of things. She and Roger were both talented and hard-working but Elaine was senior to Roger. The job was rightfully hers. But he was given the promotion and the women at the store were up in arms.

'It's so unfair!' they exclaimed, over coffees in the Arco. 'Now that Caroline's left, there's not one display manager who's a woman. It's all blokes. Look at us working like morons. We'll never get promoted.'

It was true. Roger was a great friend and I didn't begrudge him a promotion, but it was clear that the male Mafia at Harrods wasn't going to let women get ahead easily. After talking about it, Danielle, Fiona and I went to our union representative to complain about sex discrimination.

The next day a senior manager took me to one side. 'You're

doing well, Mary,' he said. 'But I don't want you to get involved in this and put your chances of promotion at risk.'

Within twenty-four hours, I'd joined about a dozen female Harrods employees who marched up and down on the pavement outside the store in protest. The head of personnel came down to try to persuade us to stop but we had union rights. Then the manager tried another tack and said that I no longer had to report to Paul Falvey: I could officially be in charge of the Way In display and windows. I still didn't shut up but our protest wasn't enough. The union failed to address the problem, most women at the store were too scared of making any fuss to join us and Roger moved up the ladder.

By now, Way In was full of activity, hosting a big launch of a new Mary Quant make-up line, for which I'd piled paint pots and brushes in a window I'd painted purple, and a fashion show. Even as Britain went to war in the Falklands, the luxury world of Harrods kept forging ahead, like an ocean liner unaffected by choppy currents. A catwalk was put up across the department floor, and in a flurry of choreography, hair and make-up, dressing models and making sure the music was right, I sent everyone down the catwalk. Barbara was cool and collected and I worked to show her that I could be, too – for almost the first time in my life. It was a great opportunity and I took charge of the look of the show, dressing the models identically to the mannequins in store. As customers watched them come down the catwalk in next season's fashions, it was as if the mannequins had come to life.

But, even so, Caroline's departure and the fiasco over her successor had left me and other people wondering about the future. Soon Fiona had also resigned and started freelancing as a window dresser. Coming home from work, I'd find her making props at the kitchen table and chatting about what she'd done that day.

Everything was changing and I envied Fiona's freedom and the fact that she was making her own way in the world, away from a company where opportunities to move upwards seemed limited. But I still wasn't sure if this was enough to make me want to leave the safety of Harrods. Having known extreme financial insecurity, I was terrified of it, and although I didn't earn much, I at least had a regular wage. I decided to stick to what I knew and make a bit extra on the side selling bric-à-brac at markets with Fiona on the weekends.

But one day I was inside a Way In window touching up a display when there was a knock on the glass. This wasn't an infrequent occurrence and I usually turned to find some bloke with his crotch squidged against the window. I ignored it. But the person on the other side of the glass wouldn't give up and I eventually turned around.

It was only Malcolm bloody McLaren. He was standing on the pavement in a big overcoat and a Buffalo hat, gesturing at me to come outside. I climbed out of the window and went over to him.

'I've been watching your windows,' he said, in a distinctive drawl. 'Pretty out there, aren't they? I'm surprised Harrods lets you get away with it.'

'Friends in high places,' I said, and he smiled at me.

'What do you do with your props when you're finished with them? I've got a shop in World's End. I need props. Here's my card. Tell them I sent you.'

He gave me his card before walking away. A few days later I visited his store and sold the manager a couple of props that I'd bought from Harrods because they were no longer needed. As I got on the train back to Sudbury Hill, I realized that everyone was moving on and I'd be left behind if I didn't, too. Malcolm had got me thinking. He always was good at stirring things up.

Spitfire

Fiona stands beside me, staring at the window. 'It's good,' she says.

'Thanks.'

'Your first day as a freelance. We've got to celebrate!'

We're standing outside Pinto's on the King's Road. I've just dressed one of its windows after leaving Harrods. I tested the water about finding new work while I was still there by asking around for some extra. The Sheraton Park Tower Hotel had paid me thirty-seven pounds and a free cocktail every week to dress their retail display cases. A guy from Harrods who'd gone to work at Piccadilly Sports had asked me to help out on their display, and I'd got thirty pounds for the few hours it took to do each week. But Way In had given me a taste for fashion that I didn't want to give up so I'd gone into Pinto's to ask if they needed help. When they agreed to employ me freelance to do their display, I knew the time had come to make the break from Harrods.

I needed transport, though, if I was going to move around London from shop to shop with props and kit. Graham had added to the small amount of money I had saved and I'd been sensible: I'd bought a bright orange Spitfire that was so tiny I was permanently driving around with mannequins' legs sticking out of the passenger window.

Fiona and I cross the road and get into the car. It's a hot summer's evening and we wind down the windows.

'So, are we going to celebrate?' Fiona asks.

'I think we should.'

'Where?'

'Corks.'

'That wine bar in South Kensington?'

'Yeh. Graham said he'd meet me there. I spent ten minutes in a phone box earlier, trying to get through to him at work to arrange it, and there's no way of letting him know if we want to go somewhere else.'

'That's fine. Let's go there.'

I switch on the radio. 'Every Little Thing She Does Is Magic' by the Police is playing. Fiona smiles at me.

'That's about right,' she says, with a giggle.

I turn to her. 'Did you really like the window?'

'Yes, Mary! Now, will you shut up? I know it's scary going out on your own but we're going to be fine. This is just the beginning.'

We smile slowly at each other. Then we start to laugh. Pulling out of the parking space, I turn up the stereo and start to drive along the King's Road.

Acknowledgements

Michael, Tish, Joe and Lawrence for opening up your hearts. Megan for holding my hand in your caring and talented one. And to my family: Melanie, Mylo, Verity and Horatio. What more could this Shopgirl want? I love you.

Index

265